For Aubrey Holzman —
Here it begins —
to wonder

Rennie Jones

"Directing Pierre's play *The Symmetry* was a fascinating experience. Pierre's play has so many levels from the human to the divine that we were continually delving into ourselves to find the inner truths. Looking back, I am grateful that I was given the opportunity to work with such beautiful prose."

Rose London, Director of the play *The Symmetry*

"Somewhere in the middle of the process, I realized that I was no longer the same person I had been when the original talk had taken place. It was very enlightening to 'act' like the person in the play and be able to see how the talk had transformed my thinking! Philosophical Midwifery assists us to discover what it is that we believe and why we believe what we believe; for unless we challenge ourselves, we won't find out what it is that is stopping us from reaching our most personally meaningful goals."

Julie Postel from her *Forward to The Symmetry*

"Well, just hold fast to something, catch your breath, and we will go on together. Consider, then, that each and every thing when taken by itself and in itself is something apart from what it may have or possess. Then, each one in all there is can be understood as a one such as we have described, and in that sense is no different from what we mean when we say God is One, which, of course, would be a pure One."

(said by Sophron in *Birthing a Prayer*)

"…it is often the case that one can be religious without having a spiritual life, and have a spiritual life without being connected to any religion. Religion binds people together under a belief that is believed to be a saving power. It does not require the believer to discover meaning nor to practice a discipline for reaching more profound states of Being, or mind…. The spiritual is to use the mind to see the mind and in reaching beyond it to recognize its source."

The character Pierre [from *Plato's Parmenides as the Paradigm…*]

Five Philosophical Dialogues

The Symmetry

Birthing a Prayer

Being, the One

Plato's Parmenides as the Paradigm for Metaphysics and Theology

Hellenism and Madhyamika Buddhism: A Dialogue on the Dialectic

Also by Pierre Grimes:

Is It All Relative?
[ISBN Soft 978-0-9648191-3-9]

Philosophical Midwifery: A New Paradigm for Understanding Human Problems with Its Validation,
co-authored with Regina Uliana, Ph.D.
[ISBN Hard 978-0-9648191-2-2, Soft 978-0-9648191-1-5]

Both of the above available through all book dealers.

———————

The Philosophical Path of Dreams and Daydreams
Available at *http//www.lulu.com*

*See page 182 for additional publications
and presentations by Dr. Grimes.*

Five Philosophical Dialogues

by

Pierre Grimes, Ph.D

The Symmetry

—

Birthing a Prayer

—

Being, the One

With a Translation of *Parmenides' Poem*
by William Uzgalis, Ph.D.

—

Plato's Parmenides as the Paradigm for Metaphysics and Theology

—

Hellenism and Madhyamika Buddhism:
A Dialogue on the Dialectic

Lulu

Copyright ©2009 by Pierre Grimes
All rights reserved. No part of this book may be reproduced in any form or by any means in any media without permission in certified form from the author.

Address Correspondence to:

pierre@openingmind.com
or
pierre@academyofplatonicstudies.com

**Grimes, Pierre, Ph.D.
Five Philosophical Dialogues**
The Symmetry; Birthing a Prayer; Being, the One;
Plato's Parmenides as the Paradigm for Metaphysics
and Theology; Hellenism and Madhyamika Buddhism:
A Dialogue on the Dialectic; Appendices

ISBN: 978-0-557-07655-0

Published by: Lulu.com

About the Characters: The Symmetry *is based on actual events, and Part Three of that dialogue is an edited transcript of an actual event. Otherwise, the characters in the dialogues in this book are not intended to portray specific persons.*

The cover and book were designed by Bill Gilbert. The cover design uses a modified version of the fractal by A. Montgomery used in the flyer by Allison Foust for the performances of The Symmetry *in Los Angeles and Huntington Beach, California, October 29 through November 13, 2002.*

Thanks to Nancy Grimes and Ronda Gilbert who checked and re-checked text, layout, references and made valuable suggestions which are integrated into this final production.

Contents

How I Met Him ix
Forward to The Symmetry x

THE SYMMETRY 1

PART 1: JOSEPH AND RAYMOND 1
PART 2: DION, MIKE, STEVE, HARRY, SUSAN, & SOPHRON 10
PART 3: SOPHRON AND JULIE WITH OTHERS 32
PART 4: SOPHRON AND HARRY 65
PART 5: RAYMOND AND JOSEPH 70

BIRTHING A PRAYER 76

BEING, THE ONE 90

Author's Introduction 91
SCENE 1: EROTIMA'S INTRODUCTION 95
SCENE 2: DIALOGUE WITH EROTIMA AND GLAUCON 96
SCENE 3: EROTIMA'S RECOLLECTION 100
SCENE 4: PARMENIDES AND THE GODDESS:
                  PARMENIDES' POEM 102
SCENE 5: DIALOGUE WITH PHILOLAUS AND GLAUCON 106
SCENE 6: EROTIMA CONCLUDES 124
Selected Bibliography 126

PLATO'S PARMENIDES AS THE PARADIGM
     FOR METAPHYSICS AND THEOLOGY 129

References 164

HELLENISM AND MADHYAMIKA BUDDHISM:
     A DIALOGUE ON THE DIALECTIC 166

Bibliographical Sources from Thomas McEvilley 174

Appendix 1: Philosophical Midwife Talk Notes   176
Appendix 2: Images in Words   178
Also by Pierre Grimes–for reference   182

You! You are a man! You have a voice. Speak your mind, for meaningful sounds have been awaited since immeasurable time. Give voice to the vision of Man. And through continual questioning and reflection may you polish to a brilliance that which illuminates the soul and so ends the dark silence of the Ages.

                                                       A. Finsky

How I Met Him

Flames roared inside of the kiln firing some pottery we had made. Distinctive looking people mostly in their twenties were standing around chatting and laughing—long hair, mostly sandals, bell-bottom pants, beards. Some artists, some not. It was the midsixties, and a lot was changing in American society, and I was changing, too.

Then a tall fellow walked up with a short haircut, horn rimmed glasses, clean shaven, nice shoes, slacks and a short sleeve sport shirt. He looked to be in his thirties. Quite different.

"How's your world?" he asked. For some reason you knew his question was sincere. In the now nearly silent group–all of whom had turned toward him–several murmured mostly empty comments such as "Fine." "How are you?" "Doing fine." It was a most curious question–not easy to answer adequately.

Anyway, we all went into the house, and they all gathered around this fellow. I still had no idea who he was. It was a small house in which the kitchen, dining area and living room seemed to huddle around a central fireplace. The newcomer sat at the table visible to everyone, but not everyone could see all the others. I was squatting, Native American style, on the kitchen floor about 6 feet away.

I don't know exactly how it began, but somehow this fellow was talking to me, asking me questions, but I was asking him questions as well, mostly about words to be sure of the terms he was using. I wish I could recall that particular conversation, but I am quite sure it was about Love, lovers and nonlovers. And I am fairly sure we touched on Beauty. Much of our talk I'm sure can be found in Plato's *Phaedrus*.

He and I were alone together. It was as if no one else was there but him and me. People, walls, even the physical being of the fellow I was talking to were not there. I was not aware of my body. We were the ideas we were questioning and examining. The ideas came from within me, and I was not willing to let a point go by that I didn't understand clearly. I felt totally open with the fellow asking for a repeat or clarification when I didn't understand–to which he freely responded.

Then, someone's voice broke in and said, "I guess I'd better introduce you. Bill? This is Doctor Grimes. You will have him for philosophy next semester. Doctor Grimes, this is Bill Gilbert."

I don't know how I knew, but there in that group he and I shared a special sort of relationship. I had just completed my first year of college in my mid-twenties, and I knew he was not the usual "professor" or "doctor" with a bunch of "knowledge" that he would try to give me. Here was a man who wished to explore together with the person whatever they talked about. He wanted to see what I saw, and when I didn't see as well as I could have, he was the sort of a friend who didn't tell me what to see, but show me how to look to see it for myself.

That was the first time I met Pierre Grimes. I am quite sure you will find in these dialogues the kind of insight with which you can grow in your life as I have in my dialogues with him. I wish you well in your journey.

Bill Gilbert

Forward to The Symmetry

by Julie Postel

As we stood waiting for our public transportation to the airport, Pierre said to me, "If you transcribe that talk we had, I will write a play around it." "Hmmm," I thought, "what a great opportunity to see even more than I did during the exploration," since it had been so unusual. The exploration had been a philosophical midwife talk during which Pierre assisted me in discovering the state of mind and attendant false belief which were causing me such physical distress in the present. I had flown to Carson City, Nevada to participate in a small workshop with Pierre as he demonstrated the Art of Philosophical Midwifery to a class of students from the Science of Mind. Helen and Steve Schmidt had invited Pierre to show his method as an extension of their work with him through the Holmes Institute. When I came into the workshop with a splitting headache, Pierre took the opportunity to take me through an exploration while also discussing each step along the way with those listening. Because I wasn't a novice to Pierre's non-interpretive method for exploring our blocks, I was able to sit and listen as he told the group about the principles of Philosophical Midwifery. But could Pierre actually assist me to discover a belief which was related to having a headache, I wondered?! I had never seen Pierre take a physical phenomenon and relate it to states of mind.

It was such a unique talk in Carson City that I wasted no time in presenting Pierre with the transcription. The amazing thing is what he did with it! He wrote the play, "The Symmetry," which turns out to capture not only a picture of my condition at the time, but he also provides a glimpse into many of our societal belief systems. The play was so interesting that Pierre was offered the challenge of having it performed for some meetings of the Science of Mind . He took the challenge, wrote a screenplay version, and extended the same challenge to our community to participate. Several of us auditioned for the roles, and I took the challenge to memorize the key monologue of my character's part of the play and won the opportunity to play my character and memorize the rest of my part. It is fascinating to me that I was able to slip into that role each time we performed the play, and the achievement itself became an example of my challenge of my false beliefs.

The other roles were played by other longtime students of Pierre. We performed the play six times for the public, and because of the excellent direction of Rosemary London, and the dedication of Nancy Grimes to holding us to the words, we were able to pull it off! Somewhere in the middle of the process, I realized that I was no longer the same person I had been when the original talk had taken place. It was very enlightening to "act" like the person in the play and be able to see how the talk had transformed my thinking! Philosophical Midwifery assists us to discover what it is that we believe and why we believe what we believe; for unless we challenge ourselves, we won't find out what it is that is stopping us from reaching our most personally meaningful goals. For when we pursue something beyond our practical goals, we are forced to challenge any belief about ourselves which is incompatible with either the goal or maintaining it. We cannot believe ourselves to be stupid and then attain to a goal which shows us to be brilliant!

Is it possible to study belief in general by studying a personal exploration? Is it possible to see that similar dynamics are operating throughout any form of belief? Pierre Grimes has brought what may be all the major belief systems together into one room and we hear their world views and then see a personal exploration as part of the play which reveals the underlying cause of a particular belief and demonstrates the method for doing so; we see a grand symmetry in the workings of the mind and in the method Pierre Grimes has developed for exploring the blocks to the attainment and maintenance of our highest personally meaningful goals.

To see that we are intelligible beings even in our times of folly is something worth seeing, and Pierre Grimes throughout his 50-year career has demonstrated again and again that our problems are resolvable, that we are able to understand both the physical and mental components of human behavior in terms of his method which has its roots in the Platonic tradition. Please visit http://www.openingmind.com for more information on Pierre's work and see for yourself that you can understand yourself without interpretation. Perhaps by reading this play, you will get a glimpse of yourself in one of the characters and wonder how it is that we can appear to have so much in common with a group and yet each be walking around with a prejudice, a false belief, which dominates our way of being and prevents us from entering into a clear state of mind. And what's more, Pierre's work has shown that each individual must see for himself in the particular events of life how the belief was taken on and that we can figure it out and why. It's worth doing. It is the noblest game, as Pierre is so fond of saying.

This play, "The Symmetry" is as valuable to me now as when the first draft was handed to me by Pierre Grimes. At first it was important because he thought it was valuable, but as the process unfolded, it was obvious that the benefit from memorizing and working with others was also mine. And as I have challenged myself to reach higher and higher goals, other aspects of the specific past scenes studied in the play have been revealed, and my life continues to be better and better. I have certainly benefited from Philosophical Midwifery, and I believe those who also participated in this great experiment would agree with me in expressing gratitude to Pierre Grimes. I am grateful to Rosemary London: Director, Nancy Grimes: Casting and On Book, and actors Michael Cox, Barbara Stecker, Julie Hoigaard, Darlene Anderson, Ronda Gilbert, William Gilbert, Kevin Gray, Ingmar Northcott, Josh Bean and Regina Uliana.

And, oh, my name at the time of the play was Julie Grabel. The changes I was able to make in my thinking through Philosophical Midwifery created the condition for me to meet and develop a mature relationship with the man I married in 2007. I have also been able to write and present papers at philosophical conferences, and philosophy has become a way of life.

The Symmetry

A Dialogue for the Noetic Society's Study of Plato's Parmenides

Part 1: Joseph and Raymond

Joseph: I think I can give a pretty good account of the conference you are asking about. I wasn't there, but I heard a good account of it from Helen. She was there with Gail and Gil and they hosted the meeting at their Church of Religious Science in Carson City, Nevada. By the way, the talk you are inquiring about took place several years ago, so I guess there are some people just like you who are drawn to it and want to know more about it. What awoke your interest?

Raymond: I guess I never cared too much about the talks going on around here, and the few I have been in never seemed to go anywhere that I thought worth the effort. But when I heard about this meeting, I knew I should learn more about it. As you know, I soft peddled the claims that it is possible to truly know yourself through some intellectual speculating. I'd say I felt double about a church affair that stresses belief and at the same time is pushing the use of the mind. I've known people in that church and even looked over their bible, *Science of Mind*, and while I can admit there were parts of it I liked, it didn't prove that mind could become an object of science.

Joseph: As I recall, weren't you the one who was laughing around town about a church with an impossible name, holding conferences on an absurd topic? And if I recall, I do think that you have said that the whole affair was nothing but an oxymoron squared. So tell me what has caused your shift?

Raymond: Well, it is simple; since the Church of Religious Science believes it is possible to create a religious science, I figured that if they had the balls to open their doors to the kind of talks your group gets into that I just ought to find out what's going on with your group and that church.

Joseph: Your answer avoided the fact that it took you a few years to hear it. So what did you hear that awoke you from your slumbers?

Raymond: Some of the ideas that were explored there I have had to see in a new way. So now I have to admit they have caught my interest, and some of them have caused me to wonder about their implications. Sure I have heard them before, but I put them aside; only now I believe I ought to take another look at them. You seem to know the most about them, so I wanted a chance to hear about them from you.

Joseph: Say, are you planning on writing another article for the New Perspectives Journal, or is there also something else at work within your soul?

Raymond: Maybe. But each time I hear about it I get different accounts. Your name keeps coming up, and I have been told that you have been playing a curious role in all this. Now, I know you are not above adding a bit of your own to a story to kind of dress it up, right? Because I remember you saying that you used to add a few lines of your own to the roles that you played on the stage. I figured your additions just might make it more fun and maybe easier to grasp.

Joseph: You are right, I have done that, but I don't need to add anything of mine to some of these talks. Choose then, what do you prefer: Is it a summary of what has been happening, or do you just want to hear about this last Church of Religious Science conference? It's up to you.

Raymond: Why not fill me in about the conference and add whatever you think I might need to better grasp what's truly been going on? And now what about your role?

Joseph: You're right. I have been into these ideas, explored them often, and now I not only give talks but I run some meetings and workshops myself. However, Raymond, when I give a talk about these conferences I might add something here and there to emphasize certain ideas, but I try my best to represent the ideas as accurately as I can. Actually, there are parts of the conferences, especially the dialogues, that I don't need to add or accent anything at all to because they have a kind of unity and precision to them that deserves telling them just as they happened.

Raymond: You graduated, what do you know, so now you are a teacher. Well, if the last conference includes a dialogue, I'd really like to hear an account of it because I really need to get a better picture of this dialogue stuff. I knew it had been going on around here, but I never got caught up in it until now.

Joseph: As for my being a teacher, I wouldn't call what I do teaching because teachers tell, and what I mostly do is demonstrate, not teach. In either case, I am glad to have the opportunity since it gives me another chance to reflect upon what it is I'm doing. I'll tell you something curious. You might not believe it, but I have found reflecting and retelling these ideas brings me to a deeper realization of what understanding really is.

Raymond: So you've become some sort of spokesman for this group, right? I just meant that you seem to have gotten off on this stuff, and I never pictured you as that kind of a guy. Now don't let that get you upset. Shall I say you are in the guru game? Now, you spend more time with a coffee cup in your hand and talking to people about what's on their minds; I just don't get the turn around. As for the conferences, I'm very interested in the one that Sophron, Ionia, and Julie were at because it sure seems to have got a few of our friends into talking.

Joseph: Sure enough. And you are right about my getting off on it, and I hope for more. When a conference is announced on dreams and Platonic thought, those are the people who are most likely to show up. I can fill you in on some of them later if you care to hear about them. I have been to some workshops that show the interrelationship between dreams, daydreams, and philosophical midwifery. Say Raymond, have you ever looked at your own dreams? Wouldn't it be something if your dreams mirrored your interest in these kinds of things and challenge you to go deeper into these ideas?

Raymond: Hold it! I don't want to go into that dream stuff. You know what though? I would like to hear this account of yours so why not fill me in. I believe I may have been standing on the periphery for too long. Besides I am also interested in learning why some people are getting attracted to these ideas. So if you are into it I would like to hear as much as you would like to give, so why not sit back and recall the conference and anything else that seems to you to fit in with that subject you mentioned?

Joseph: Do you know that what you're asking about will take a bit of time?

Raymond: That's fair; I have plenty of time. Would you clue me in on how it all started?

Joseph: Sure. Helen told me how her part in all this began. I'll tell it as Helen told me, and as I recall the conference I might weave in parts from other talks that I think you just might enjoy hearing. I see you are taking notes. Better watch out, Raymond. That's just how I started.

She began her story with a brief account of how she met Sophron at a Holmes Institute Conference that the Church of Religious Science sponsored for their divinity students. You know, for those who were interested in entering the ministry? She said she had taken his philosophy course at the Institute, and he was there to do some workshops at the Conference. It turned out that he gave a talk about how he had adapted Socratic midwifery and was using it for exploring the kind of personal problems we have to face when we push for excellence in something worthwhile and important to us. As you probably have heard, the idea of midwifery is a way of dialoguing with another person to assist them in giving birth to the ideas that puzzle and block them. Helen told me that what got to her was the way he accepted a problem a student volunteered and took that student through a midwifery session right there.

Well, she said that she contacted him later and discussed a problem she was having; and in a few exchanges this philosopher guy brought her to see what really was at the root of her problem, and she broke out of it.

Raymond: I sure would like to know how he did that. I know her. She lives in Carson City. I guess she had to travel a lot to see him get that kind of result.

Joseph: No. He did it through e-mail exchanges, that's what.

Raymond: Do you really believe that's how?

Joseph: I haven't seen the e-mails if that's what you mean. That's what I heard. Believe it or not, that's up to you.

Raymond: That comes close to being magic, you know. It adds to the problem of having to believe what is said about Sophron. Anyhow tell your story your way.

Joseph: As the story goes this philosopher, Sophron, was invited to give a workshop exploring these ideas of midwifery, and he turned it into a personal exploration for those who were interested in delving into either their dreams or their personal problems. During the weekend he gave a sermon on "the Shadows on the Wall of the Mind." And after the sermon he followed it up with a guided meditation on the nature of those shadows. It was curious because he said that they are images of beliefs projected on the wall by a fire or luminosity that was man-made. The beliefs are false beliefs about what it is to be truly a Man.

Raymond: He pushed Plato a bit further, you know?

Joseph: It was mind boggling; because with each person he engaged in dialogue he was able to show they unknowingly believed some fiction about themselves as if it were true. With each it opened the door into more profound ways of experiencing a new way of understanding themselves. He used the same method, the same questions, over and over again, in his dialoguing with others—only adapted them to the individual.

Raymond: An image can't see or hear. Did it go any further?

Joseph: He varied the questions slightly to meet the needs of the individual that he was dialoguing with, and nearly all reached an interesting state of mind. Those present agreed that he showed the same interest in one and all and was able to bring each individual to new understanding of himself.

Raymond: Yes, I have heard about this before, only I have to admit that it is not easy to accept that I have a false belief about myself that I don't know I have. It just doesn't make any sense that a person's blocks or problems are caused by some unsuspected belief that they have.

Joseph: You can see it for yourself. You know you don't have to believe me since the sessions were all audio-taped and you can hear them for yourself.

Raymond: I heard about it, only I thought that on the face of it that it was a typical case of exaggeration and enthusiasm, so I ignored it. Sometime later I met your friend Kathy; she told me that she volunteered for one of those sessions, and it turned into a philosophical midwife talk. She said that Sophron went to the heart of a problem she didn't even know she had, that he was able to get to the very core of her deep seated emotional problem. She said that he showed her how those false beliefs were planted. Now that is something! He did it, and now she is doing it to others. Seeing her and hearing her say that to my face convinced me I ought to find out what is going on. I knew the old Kathy and she certainly has grown. Actually, she has left me behind and I don't like it. There are some things I do that she pokes fun at. So please tell me about the conference.

Joseph: That is fair, Raymond. After that first conference at Gail and Gil's church, the philosopher Sophron was asked by Helen if he would give a critique of the church's services that he had just witnessed. He turned everything around and said that since he didn't really know what a prayer should be, he couldn't very well judge what they were doing when they were praying. He said that he wasn't even sure that the prayer Socrates offered at the end of one of Plato's dialogues was a prayer or not. Someone had brought a copy of Plato so everyone heard it read aloud several times, and as you might imagine nothing was settled and a general kind of confusion took over.

To top that off he added to the confusion when he said that the ideas he heard expressed in the church sermon were like beautiful colors an artist might use to paint his creation in a carefree and spontaneous manner. All this sounded beautiful, only he added that the paintings he preferred were those in the style of Raphael or Rembrandt because with them the colors had to fit most artfully, and had to match the life-like creations they were painting. He was saying that the words would really have to fit into some meaningful whole otherwise one might conclude that they are like the paintings of that creative artist when he was expressing himself spontaneously but without regard to any object.

After that he raised an interesting question: What kind of church service would there be if all the words that were uttered fit into a meaningful context? Do you appeal to the heart or the mind? Can there be an uplifting rational discourse that would serve the needs of those who want a sermon? What would it be like? Strangely enough, he went on to explain that if there was such a discourse or sermon it would most likely follow a Platonic model and most likely be based on Plotinus' works.

Raymond: You're not kidding, are you? What else did he say?

Joseph: He said that if any service was to be meaningful it would have to be metaphysically sound, and those participating in the service would naturally be drawn along a path that would bring them into a higher and more profound way of being. It would be something that might be harmonious with each person's level of development. Consider this: if it's simple and you understand it simply, then you know what is there for you; but even if you only understand the profound simply, you know that there is more there for you to understand.

Raymond: Now that is astonishing, I don't know whether to laugh or not. The Church of Religious Science would become Platonic. Do I get that right? Come one and all. We'll sing praises to Athena and instead of "hymns" we will call them "hers" and say "Ah, women" instead of "amen."

Joseph: Well, that's about it. After I heard about it, I was told that Ernest Holmes was not alone in turning to Plato and Plotinus because that ancient direction actually was the source of many European Renaissances and spiritual revivals. When Sophron mentioned this he said that his own teacher could present this Platonic view much better than he could. He said he was still studying Proclus and that his teacher might be persuaded to come to one of these conferences.

Raymond: So Sophron, the philosopher, was only a philosophical midwife and not up to the challenge, right? And that's when his teacher came into the act? Never heard of this guy, Plotinus. What is he all about? And what is the name of the Sophron's teacher?

Joseph: He made clear that the journey of the soul that Plotinus describes can be understood in terms of a rational system. Proclus is another of those Platonic philosophers that worked out a rational system. He set it out like the propositions of Euclid. I've just gotten into it and it's good. I'll tell you that, it *is* good.

Raymond: So that's how he showed up. Now, what did you say his name was? And what did you see in what went on?

Joseph: He is from Southern Italy, Velia, which was an ancient Greek colony, and his real name is a long one, Sophronicus, but everyone calls him Sophron. Other than that I don't know too much about him. They did add that they learned later that his father, Pyres, was also called Ouliades Physikos, which they said meant that he was in a lineage of sages of some sort. In any case, he was into dialogue and dreams.

Raymond: Let's see if I understand what you are stating. You are trying to understand the monstrous absurdity of man's unpredictable and irrational behavior through the study of what he least understands. Do I understand it rightly?

Joseph: Call it what you will, but what if there is a symmetry behind man's behavior and his dreams? Or Raymond, what if they both emerge out of a symmetry?

Raymond: Just because a garbage truck has fleas doesn't mean it can fly.

Joseph: It has been known for some years that a lineage of sages has applied dream analysis to human problems.

Raymond: That's a nice romantic myth to tell children; we both know that even if there were such sages, they sure didn't pass it on to someone else. Come on now. Do you really believe that kind of stuff is like the same fire persists if it is started from the embers of the old dying fire.

Joseph: It has been known for some time that a lineage of sages did exist for hundreds of years in Velia, and they developed a method of dream analysis that seemed to work when applied to man's condition.

Raymond: Let's see now, you are trying to understand the continuous absurdity of man's behavior by making an analysis of his nightmares. Do I get that right? The record of man's unpredictable and irrational behavior will be made perfectly clear by interpreting what no one understands. Is that right?

Joseph: Call it what you will; that's your right. Why not deal with the possibility that there just might be an inner rationality behind all this chaos? Don't laugh it off. Why can't there be an inner pattern we are struggling to realize? What if there is a symmetry of meaning that lies behind our dreams that can illuminate even our darkest struggles?

Raymond: No matter how high you pile the rhetoric, it is still rhetoric. Let me tell you something: Wouldn't you agree that just because a cat gives birth to six kittens in an oven, that sure doesn't make them into a half a dozen biscuits, does it?

Joseph: Listen. Helen and Steve contacted Sophron, and they discussed the importance of the role of the mind in the spiritual life of the members of a religious community. How Sophron might explore this issue was left to him. He was interested in learning what conflicts the members of our church community experienced in introducing more mind in their affairs, and he wanted to understand those who objected to the idea. He told them that unless the function of mind is understood, there can be no harmony within a spiritual community; and without that, no man can catch a glimpse of his destiny. He agreed to discuss with our group his views about dreams and man's destiny. Now, the idea took off and some applauded it and others rejected it believing that love and friendship is all one needs to conquer all problems. Several of them said they wanted to share their views about this idea, so after the date was selected, it was agreed to follow the symposium model. Recall Plato's *Symposium*? He described how friends gathered to celebrate

Agathon's winning a prize for his play, and with all that good cheer they agreed that each of the participants should be given the opportunity to give a full dress oration in praise of Love.

Raymond: I like that, I really do. You have gained some fame for writing plays, so why not set it out as a play so I can imagine myself in the front seat.

Joseph: That's a good idea. When I think it is right, I can improvise to weave it all together. I'll give it my best try.

THE SYMMETRY, PART 2:
DION, MIKE, STEVE, HARRY, IONIA, AND SOPHRON

Joseph: The conference was arranged, people came, and those who wanted to express their views sat around in a circle. Actually, Raymond, you knew most of those who spoke; there was Dion, Mike, Ionia, who I don't think you know, Helen, Steve, Helen's husband, your friend Harry, and Julie, who arrived late. Each spoke, moving from left to right, until it landed on Sophron. He was then given the opportunity to proceed in any way he chose. Since Dion was sitting to the left of Sophron, he started off the discussion. He got up to talk. He walked as he talked, in a kind of reflective stance and occasionally made notes on a flip-chart, pausing here and there as if thinking out loud his innermost thoughts. He began slowly, stressing each word.

Dion: "I have been caught in a kind of theological double bind. As some of you know I was a seminarian; I was on track to become a Catholic priest; that is until I saw the rock my faith rested upon crumbled under the weight of my own attempts at scholarship. This may sound complicated but it's not.

When I talk before groups such as this one, I am confronted by a certain reluctance that I have to overcome because what I shall share with you may undermine much of what you may believe. Perhaps, I should keep it to myself because once you understand this simple truth you will discover, as I have, that much falls away and you won't know if you are better off for the loss or not. Well, I have started so I shall put caution aside and continue. This may sound complicated but it is not. Please consider one idea and it is a simple idea that governs all theological study and that is the idea of likelihood.

First, let me review a few things. Scholars have dated the sayings of Jesus to be about 50 A.D. And these sayings are found in both the Gospel of Matthew and Luke. It is argued that these sayings served the needs of the first group of followers of Jesus. These sayings are called "Q." Is it likely that the material that was added to Q was essential to the message of Jesus yet was not included in the teaching until some 30 years later? Scholars and theologians now are exploring the interesting similarity between a contemporary group of philosophers who closely resemble the way they confronted social ills, their style of life, their dress, and ethics and the way Jesus functioned and how he told his own disciples to live. These philosophers were centered in Gadara, a short distance from Nazareth. A close look at the parallels between the Jesus movement and these philosophers has convinced more than one theologian that the early Christian movement was akin to the style of life and teaching of these philosophers.

The important issue of the Gospel of Thomas is that it, like the Q material, has no mention of the transfiguration, nor the arrest, nor the trial, nor the crucifixion, nor the resurrection; nor does he mention the founding of a church by the apostles. Is it likely that both Thomas and the writers of Q knew of these events but simply ignored them? Or that they were added later to make a religion out of a teaching? Now since the Gospel of Thomas was circulating about the time Mark wrote his gospel but before the other gospels were written is it likely that they chose to add what Thomas and Q ignored? Or is it more likely that these other synoptic Gospel writers found a need to add a drama to those teachings and turned to the Hellenistic mystery cult teachings, Gnostic mythology, and Jewish apocalyptic teachings to produce what we now call Christianity?

Or if this message is only in Paul then they are Pauline and not synoptic gospel followers. What does that mean? It means the last gospel to be written was John, somewhat around 100 A.D., and only there do we find somewhat of a correspondence with Paul's teaching. See, it is a question of likelihood, isn't it? Let me put it simply: If all of this has been added, then is it more likely that Christianity as we know it today was made by the church in the fourth century by carefully selecting only those documents that could support their own view of a church system? Is it likely or not, then, that the present state of Christianity is a man-made religion? And that those early communities that the Gospel of Thomas and Q served are of a different breed than modern churches? And which is it more likely that Jesus served?

For myself, what I have found and reflected upon leads me to believe that the teachings of Jesus turned out to be St. Paul's end run around the ministry of Jesus. Simply put, Paul's teaching cannot be found in the synoptic gospels. When I saw that, it suddenly occurred to me that I ought to stop referring to Paulism as Christianity and call it simply the doctrine of Paul.

The church made the writings of Paul the cornerstone of their faith, and they read all else through the eyes of Paul. It came to a crisis point for me when I realized that what the earliest gospel of Mark is saying is that Jesus taught the multitude in parables to keep them from discovering the meaning of his teaching, "lest they should turn again and be forgiven," while he taught his own disciples how to understand the parables. He insisted that they understand, not believe. He wanted his inner circle to understand not only the parables but also the significance of what he was doing through his miracles and his acts. You can easily see this for yourself. Take the time to figure out what the Gospel of Mark means when Jesus says, "Beware of the leaven of the Pharisees and the leaven of Herod." He demands they understand not merely the significance of the feeding of the 4,000 and 5,000, but in terms of what was left over—the garbage. I realized this simple analogy:

As believers <u>are to</u> miracles

so too

Those into understanding <u>are to</u> the kingdom of God

Was the teaching that no one was teaching? I asked, but no one had worked out the meaning of all of the 32 parables, even though Jesus said that only through an understanding of the parables could one reach the kingdom of God. What does that mean? The church and maybe all Christianity followed Paul and made belief the center piece of Christianity, and in doing so rejected Jesus' urgent call to understand. Frankly, we have lost touch with whatever Jesus was doing. Paul drove a stake into the heart of the teachings he could not understand.

I knew that there were many gospels written during these early years, but they were all burned and destroyed by church authorities because, as I was told, they were not authentic. We thought them all lost, but many were recently discovered and translated. I felt a kinship with the Gospel of Thomas, that of Truth, and many others, and could only feel a grievous sadness that they were not part of the New Testament. See for yourself. Get a copy of the *Nag Hamadhi Library* at your bookstore.

What was worse was to learn that the most authentic sayings of Jesus, which theologians call Q, make no reference to Jesus' arrest, trial, crucifixion, or resurrection. The earliest Gospel, that of Mark, ended without a resurrection account—the twelve verses that cite the resurrection of Jesus were added some 300 years after the Gospel was written. If you ignore these last twelve verses, then Mark's version ends with the opening of the tomb. Without the resurrection account the focus shifts to the crucifixion account, and we are left in puzzlement with Jesus' last words, "My God, My God, Why has thou forsaken me?" because that makes the gospel a true tragedy. There is a theologian who showed how the very structure of Mark's Gospel matches Aristotle's idea of the way a tragedy should be constructed. If so, I wondered whether we ought to read Mark like we do a Greek tragedy. The midpoint of a tragedy is also its high point, its most important turning point of the drama. Looking at it in this way focuses, naturally, on the most dramatic event of the gospel, which is the story of Jesus in the midst of a divinely radiant luminosity talking with Moses and Elijah, who appeared through that light—here is a spiritual resurrection. I ask myself, "What if that luminosity is the true manifestation of God on our plane of existence? What if it is the mind itself showing itself in all its splendor?" I can't say if it happened or not. Maybe I would like to believe it. But I do know that it got me searching through other religious writings looking for other such accounts.

You know that it may not be known to many people today but the church once believed that there were two religious paths open to man and that one of them was called a partial revelation, a Platonic tradition which was based upon reason, and the other was based upon faith and the metaphysics of St. Dionysius. There were a number of theologians who held his writings to be at least equal to the Bible itself. Because in making a bridge for faith to understanding, he healed the ancient wound. Now that great system of thought was strongly held to until it was discovered that the writings of Dionysius were a hoax.

What's more, the shock of realizing the document believed to be the legal basis for the establishment of the Roman Church—called the Donation of Constantine—was a forgery brought me to a diligent study of the church's history of forgeries. What can I say? After that, I realized that more and more of church teaching was an effort to justify the continued existence of the church. The cathedrals, requiems, and all the art connected with the church is indeed beautiful but does not inspire me to devotion. What I dreaded was the thought that I would have to justify a parishioner's faith when I have a faith but I don't know what I believe.

All this left me with a burning question: Must one sacrifice one's mind to save one's soul? To save your soul can you make-believe you believe? Can you convince yourself against your own understanding that you believe when you don't? Can there really be a spiritual system that bases itself on the understanding of parables rather than belief? Is it at all possible for understanding and reason to replace belief? Can some experience confirm that kind of understanding?

Well, maybe we should shop around for a spiritual system that matches our needs like we do when we want to buy a house? Perhaps we have reached the point where we ought to open up the question of what we want to put into the Bible. Why not ask if it is at all possible to bring together all that is significant to the spiritual life of man, East and West, and make that into a spiritual system or the religion. Or build it out of the Bible, the *Nag Hamadhi Library*, Pseudo-Dionysius, and anything else that will save us from ourselves. Why do we have to fight over the authentic bits that have survived if that wasn't what made it great? Maybe I'm a little bitter and disillusioned; so when I heard there might be a discussion around here dealing with the priority of understanding over belief, I knew I had to attend. I wonder whether or not I am trying to find some spiritual system that will be courageous enough to say that to sustain all life there must be a joining of the masculine and feminine and that this union is not limited to the realm of the biological but must be part of the fabric of the universe. I'm not saying there must be a unity of opposites simply because male and female are not opposites; they are complementary aspects of one another. I know that when one can enter into a unity, one finds a union that goes beyond these distinctions, and at such times we enter into a oneness that doesn't need to deny either the male or the female. I'm not talking about some mystical union, but the heartfelt satisfaction we can find in a look and a smile and even holding on to one another. Truly it is a peace that encompasses an understanding that just being together is a wonder of miracles.

Thank you for letting me share this with you.

Joseph: *This was the talk that Dion gave as I heard it from Helen, and later I talked to him and I only added a bit to emphasize a point or two. Next came our friend Mike. You remember him from your days when he was always into science fiction and how he used to* *tell tales out of Gibbon's Decline and Fall of the Roman Empire. He started in his usual way of talking, half-serious, half in fun, provoking and rude as usual.*

Mike: As for what Dion said, I couldn't disagree more. I don't give a proverbial damn if other traditions and spiritual systems have found truth because they are irrelevant to us. Each tradition is a reflection of their own unique historical conditions, and you just can't graft a monkey's head onto a jackass without becoming an ass yourself. You know what I mean? Like, if we haven't yet discovered the truth of something, it doesn't yet exist for us. We have to discover it in our own tradition for ourselves. You can't expect an ox cart to compete in a race against a Ferrari any more than you can put on a turban and play Hindu saint because you've learned to chant in Sanskrit.

We have our own destiny to play out because we have an inherent direction to play out, and that's more than being loyal to your tribe. It means simply that we must play out the cards we have been dealt— It means we would rather go to hell in a basket woven by science than crash down the doors of heaven with satori and nirvana. You can't embrace another tradition anymore than you can let yourself believe that just because you've fallen in love with a prostitute that doesn't make her into a sweet girl of innocence.

Haven't we had enough of belief? Just take a look at all the conflicts in our world and tell me right off how many are the result of just one archaic historical force that continually enflames the fires of discord and strife. The force has great power and is unleashed whenever someone believes there is a need to justify their faith. It is only one, though it goes by different names. It has many heads—hydra-headed it is— each has a different name but only one body. Look behind those names and you'll find a sameness they all share and that's the Judaic-Christian-Islamic tradition and that came out of Persia, Zoroastrian. It is easy to understand the source of their hostility to others. Each of these systems can't stand the slightest difference because their security blanket depends upon everyone agreeing to the same precise formula for their salvation.

They experience a degree of anxiety when they engage with those who do not share their belief. For they cannot themselves believe unless someone else appears to believe what they must believe. They become intolerant of the slightest difference so that it is easy for them to ignore, dismiss, and treat as totally irrelevant those whose formulas are different from their own.

Consider it this way: Is it not curious that they are driven to be evangelical? Why this zealous effort to convert and to propagandize one's belief? Because they try to persuade others to believe that God violates the natural order of fairness and justice by granting to only some to be his chosen people, gain salvation, and gain access to heaven. This is, of course, called a supernatural belief, and to accept it, one sacrifices one's belief that the natural order is understandable in its own terms. There is a always a tension among evangelicals whenever they find the cosmos can be understood as a coherent ordered system.

Clearly, tension increases when different evangelical systems confront one another. There will be no peace until we can find a way to disbelieve them; we need to be brought to understand that it is evangelical belief that is irrelevant. Each of these evangelical religions has had their hand at the helm of the ship of state and each crashed and was crushed on the hard rocks of history. So what? Well, when any religion wages wars to either coerce belief or drive out unbelievers, they fill their own hell with their own kind. When the crowds become disillusioned with the faith, they merely continue the same game as they become true believers of Nationalism, Fascism, and Communism. If they can't join some crusade, they have to face the emptiness of their lives. Belief feeds on sacrifice; without a cause to prove to themselves that they believe, they become listless, idle and left facing the futility of their lives and the shallowness of their beliefs. Given the chance to act out their belief, they must destroy those who oppose it; otherwise, they know their belief doesn't matter.

So, as for me, I can find a home in the Church of Religious Science because they don't stick out a promise that an evangelical formula will save you. Sure, it has metaphysical truths but not supernatural truths. For to believe that the power and intelligence that manifested this entire vast and majestic Cosmos with its billions of galaxies has transformed itself into human history to benefit one tribe or people—to the exclusion of all other intelligent beings—is a supernatural belief.

Further, must one not also believe that your place in Heaven is guaranteed because you believe in this transmuted God? And what's more, doesn't buying into supernaturalism justify the slaughter of countless people and the destruction of cultures and empires simply because they reject the imposition of that belief? But our belief is metaphysical and not a supernatural belief because our belief does not assume that the God transforms himself and steps down to play a role in history for the benefit of one tribe. For this would mean the God enters into conflict with the direction that he himself had set for his creation. For if some tribe living on a planet of a solar system among billions of others in a galaxy that is itself only one among other billions of galaxies didn't obey him or didn't call him by the proper title or name, then what was providentially designed for the whole of creation would be sacrificed. Thus, ours is not a supernatural belief, and so we reject the idea that a transmuted God plays an arbitrary role in human history—and that goes double for miracles.

It is because our belief separates itself from supernatural belief systems that it offers a hope that maybe the spiritual dimension of man may one day become part of the scientific tradition and not another form of some evangelicalism. Consider the changes culture has gone through and ask yourself, "What will turn us from our path of suicide? Will it be those who need our collective death to justify their faith? Or will science find a way to reverse our destructive path before we pass into oblivion?"

The answer comes easy, doesn't it? You know what that means? Well, it means that the closest you can get to truth is to be able to— Well, I'll tell you. There have been many who sacrificed and contributed to what we are part of: You breathe the scientific spirit even if you can't describe what an algorithm is or explain what a Plank length is.

Now, it's not just a loyalty issue. It's more like laying a bet down on a horse from your own stable, since the race we are in will determine which of the traditions is purer and truly superior and which one's sacrifices were not in vain.

When the last book is written they'll praise the spirit of our scientific age as the only one that made sense of what is real and all the rest as merely speculations and myths, that's what. Of all the "isms" of this age the only one that you can trust is scientism. So where does that put me? I'll listen along with everyone else but one thing I'll always fall back on is simply this: you can say there is a science of the brain but not science of mind. I might change my thinking if it can be shown to me that mind, which I take to be something intelligible, has some existence independent of the brain. That possibility I have wondered about, I'm deeply interested in, but it will have to be shown to me, that's what.

Well, if there is to be a science of mind it would have to be able to present a model of the way mind functions, it would have to be a model that would include the way we come to know. It would have to be a mathematical model that would include the dynamics of belief, of opinion, and understanding and, maybe even of knowing. I tell you what I hope; I hope it would be like one of those hyperspace models that mathematicians created and that theoretical physicists play with when they speculate about black holes and quarks and stuff. So I guess I'm somewhat interested in what's going on here, and my wife is involved with all this, so I figure I might as well come along. You know what I mean?

Joseph: *Some of the audience were smiling a bit at the way Mike carried off his talk, some were nodding in agreement, and some were perplexed by what he had put into words. Next Steve spoke, but his approach was different than that taken by Dion and Mike. He had his own direction. As I recall he talked somewhat slowly as if he was surfacing his thoughts as he spoke.*

Steve: I would like to say what brought me here and what I hope to discover. First, I am into science. I'm in awe of it and disillusioned by it. I strongly believe that science will accomplish its dream of reaching an understanding of everything; it is what we call the TOE, the Theory Of Everything. But the theory does not include everything; it leaves man out of the equation. If everything fits into a rational model, is man left out because he is irrational? Does science stop where we need it most? Is man's rationality only a veneer or does it go deep enough to escape his destructive nihilism? What, if I may ask, does rationality mean? We can answer that in the sciences the most fundamental sign of rationality in anything or anywhere is the presence of symmetry. So when I heard from Michelle that the idea of metaphysics and spirituality was going to be explored in terms of symmetry I could not wait to sign up. But what surprised me more than that was when she said that she heard Sophron discuss the idea that symmetry was basic both to an understanding of problem solving and in the understanding of dreams. As you may know, she too has an interest in exploring dreams as a source of creativity. So I wondered what form Sophron's talk might take, how the point might be developed, so I'm here.

You see, the idea of symmetry is closely associated with the laws of physics, the special theory of relativity is based upon it, and the gravitational force embodied in relativity theory is nothing but the principle of equivalence. You find the same thing in the discoveries of the strong, weak, and electromagnetic forces; these discoveries were all based upon principles of symmetry. If you want to explain 20th century physics you just have to talk symmetry. To understand the major breakthroughs in physics you focus on one thing, and that one thing is symmetry. It was Dirac's prognosis, based upon the assumption of symmetry, that an electron had antiparticle. Take chaos theory. There you have a mathematical model that suggests that the way genes develop in their evolutionary track can be understood by symmetry in the law of self-similarity, or what is called automorphism. Consider this: Quantum entities are indeterminate, they pass through ceaseless transformations and fluxes of energy. Throughout all the transformations symmetry alone remains the same. With the discovery of any symmetry in nature, either in space or time, there is a corresponding conservation law of momentum or mass/energy. Whatever is found will always be symmetric: what was before and what was after any interaction remains the same. What is found in the subatomic order of things is not random chaos but a symmetry that is called a super—a supersymmetry. An amazing order is revealed, expressible in mathematics, confirmed in physics. Can it be found in man? Well, now I'm reading in Klaus Mainzer and he says that human knowledge and action are at their root determined by symmetry principles.

In our discussion we borrowed the term symmetry from the language of theoretical particle physics because it suggests an analogy that can be drawn with the Higgs field and, what Leon Lederman calls, the God particle. He urges consideration of a new particle, the Higgs Boson, existing at the very beginning of the big bang, having a pure symmetry, but with the cooling down of the cosmic birthing it was broken, producing such things as quarks and everything else. It is with the breaking of the symmetry that fields express themselves; they are undetectable because they are pervasive and invariant. The elementary particles gain their mass by and through this field. What if there is only a pure wisdom and it contains all that can be known and it unfolds all the ways of knowing? What if that pure wisdom unfolds through a field that we encounter as understanding and right opinion? Then that pure wisdom must exist as something intelligible and it must exist by itself. Study that and you might have a science of mind.

Knowledge-wisdom is the symmetry and it is through the field of analogical structures that ignorance, right opinion and understanding emerge and gain a mode of existence. Like these subatomic particles, each of the cognitive set presupposes knowledge and the field of analogy. In a similar manner to the Higgs Boson, knowledge does not contribute much to the everyday fashions of the world—it contributes negligibly at low energies—but its influence is massive at high levels of experience, or energy.

For me all this talk about symmetry misses the major problem. Are these symmetries our own projection? Or can they be understood as principles of self-organization, and are they in nature? If it is all our projection, then we only find what we project into. We build machines that are sensitive to our own projections, and you know what they call people who call their own projections reality. This is the issue between Stephen Hawking and Roger Penrose: Hawking says it's all our projection, Penrose that there is a reality that corresponds to our theory. If Penrose is right, then reality exhibits principles of intelligence, reality can be said to be intelligible, and we're getting close to understanding that there is an inherent beauty to the nature of reality. What is that but Plato? I would like to share with you something curious. I was brought up on the *Chronicles of Narnia*, you know, C.S. Lewis' work that the BBC filmed—at least they did parts of it. His conclusion of the Chronicles still keeps ringing in my ear, "It's all in Plato, all in Plato." I can still recall my surprise to discover that the real Narnia was therefore a Platonic Form. For Lewis to go to Plato means he saw the limits of his own tradition since no one can say Christianity embraced Plato. When I heard that Sophron talked out of that Platonic tradition, I figured I had better be part of this and hear what he was going to say about symmetry between dreams and problems. I would like to end with a quote from an often-quoted scientific sage, which indicates how far we have come from viewing nature as a random and mindless thing. Einstein said, "The most incomprehensible thing about the universe is that it is comprehensible."

> **Joseph:** *Ionia spoke next. You know her. She will be giving a talk here in a week or so. Her appearance, as usual, was striking and she engaged the audience as if she was speaking to you alone. She had that gift of talking in a quiet way, almost a whisper, and attentiveness settled in. Well, everyone knew when she got up to speak that we would hear a frank and sincere talk about psychology and love. She didn't disappoint us. As she talked she looked directly at you.*

Ionia: I would like to explain why I am here and why I wanted to share a few things with you. First, I am a matchmaker; I try to save and enrich relationships. I'm called a psychologist which means that I can get paid for talking and can advertise under a title without breaking the law.

You can study things or relationships; I study relationships. Everyone is in some kind of relationship. In order to survive in this world we enter into relationships. But few understand what a relationship really is; most are driven into it and just as fast they flee from it. The power and attraction of and into relationships is love. It is the bond that completes and binds together isolated beings, and for all its importance to the human race we still don't understand it the way we should. For all my years getting a degree there is little I learned in psych that I use in my practice. So I keep up with my reading and try to learn as I am going along.

Second, I wanted to share with you something I've found that is more than curious. I don't know where it goes but it got me here. I have tried to make sense of Love, and I mean physical love, what some people call sex, but for a long time I felt restless and didn't particularly like what I read and have heard about it. Several years ago all this changed after I had some talks with a friend. He said my difficulty was that I didn't know I was a natural Platonist. I gave him an overview of what I heard at college about Plato, and I said that Plato's doctrine that we participate in the forms, or Ideas, didn't impress me simply because it had nothing to do with my life or anyone I knew. He then asked me if my lover had to be in some special state of mind before I let him enter me. After that, he asked me how all the senses play their positive role in a sharing of essences that puts an end to any sense of being separate and apart from the object of one's love. He went on to ask if I could recall a time when our loving was most ideal and to describe what our state of mind was like at those times. He brought me to talk about what union really was. I was asked to state as best as I could what I brought to the experience that made it so profound and loving. Without my being aware of it I realized I was being gently led to see that in accepting an act of loving, I had participated and given welcome to a union that I entered into. For in loving I found what was akin to myself. I came to appreciate that none of this was possible without recognizing that I could lovingly trust my lover with myself, and my trust was vindicated as he participated with me as if entering a scared shrine.

Talking in this way about physical intimacy was new to me. Previously, I had been troubled by a suspicion that my attempt to sanctify pleasure was merely a sham act to hide from myself that I was nothing but a hedonist, a mere lover of pleasure. My friend brought me to reflect in a different way about loving. He showed me that the problem is not to escape pleasure, as if that is possible. For how could one see beauty and not find pleasure in the enjoyment of it? I was urged to see if it made a difference to hold fast to the idea that the nature of reality is truly good as one experiences pain and pleasure, fear and desire.

For myself, I see that the world of one's experience does not become good by satisfying pleasure and desire, nor does it become evil by the presence of pain and fear, rather each comes to us because our naming makes the state we entertain in our experience. The reality that allows each of these states is itself good, and in knowing that, it is possible to keep oneself from calling good and evil what are merely passing states. I'm sure some of you must have heard it discussed in Plato. It is a provocative idea, and the way he presents it makes it even more curious, because if you don't hold fast to that idea, you conclude something both the gods and men hate, which he calls the Great Lie. It is a simple idea to say, difficult to see, more difficult to put into words. But I'll tell you it is worth doing.

Given this chance to reconsider my experience brought me to a different kind of seeing. Clearly, seeing of this sort awakened me to a reality that I had only dimly perceived, and I knew seeing this sensitively is seeing with the eye of the soul as some have called it. I had been brought to see that in shifting the terms from one range of experience, love, to another, that it allowed me to see the possibility of a more profound way of seeing love and the possibility that this language was actually a shadow of the divine, an echo of the higher, and so for me it became a bridge to the higher.

The entry into the realm of meaningful love was none other than being receptive and open to the divine. You can participate in that realm because it is there that beauty emerges. Truly, it is the source of what is best in us. It is the begetter of a way of seeing that brings us to a higher state of being which we can call mindfulness. My old difficulty about the meaninglessness of Plato's participation in ideas was over as I began to realize that meaningful relationships are meaningful when we allow ourselves to participate in this very world of ideas. For each of us who has been loved has learned something about those we loved. It needs to be shared and understood or else it goes on as something unfinished and incomplete. Indeed, the intensity that brought one to embrace often obscures the reasons one's love was found beautiful, and unless those reasons are surfaced, it will remain unknown, mysterious, and a fragment of something real.

So every soul so long as it is true to itself is an Aphrodite. We have forced on one another an Apollonian ideal, but in that is our folly since Dionysus was the brother and counterpart of Apollo. Apollo is to that transformative light as Dionysus is to that power that springs from and is cultivated through erotic pleasure. In turning to that universal beauty that culminates in the Apollonian radiance we become initiated into the sublime Eros. As the erotic has been bathed in the splendor of a sincerity that emerges through mindfulness, we are no longer strangers to the divine. I have read that the primordial brilliance that created the world is no different from that divine light, and as Eliade states it so I affirm it: "The light experienced in *maithuna* is the Clear Light of Gnosis, and of Nirvanic consciousness." I would like this to be true, I have caught glimpses of its truth, I know of no one who has confirmed this experience fully or completely; but if it can become part of a genuine vision of reality, it would offer a symmetry between the sacred and the profane. Another vision of love I think is worthy of your viewing and considering is the one Jolan Chang wrote about the Tao of loving—which I will speak about later this week.

Well, it is not easy for me to say this to you, but I wanted to say that here with the Church of Religious Science we can express these ideas without the worry that we will be misunderstood and labeled falsely. There are others who are at war with these ideas, but they are not among us.

Our church is struggling to achieve a coherent vision, one that will bring the most profound vision of what it is to be human, and to offer that to society as a way to grow and to nourish the divine within us. It is my belief and hope that these ideas I have expressed will become part of the vision our Church is struggling to achieve. However, if the challenge is not taken it is inevitable that I will be part of this struggle wherever it takes me.

Joseph: *After Ionia finished her talk there was a silence and Harry got up and allowed the silence to continue for awhile. He appeared confident and ready to resume. He was about to speak, but delayed his talk when he noticed some people had arrived late and were finding places to sit. As things were settling down there was a slight commotion in the hall as a young woman named Julie made her way around the chairs to the speakers table to offer brief hellos and apologies to each of the speakers for being late. Harry took a few moments to shake hands with her and motioned for her to follow him to the far end of the table where they could both sit down. They started to discuss something with one another in hushed terms. It was as if Harry was trying to persuade her of something. Since it appeared that Harry wanted to continue his discussion with Julie he gestured to Sophron to take his turn. Sophron agreed and stood up, walked over to a flip chart and began what I later called a charted exploration. Sophron began saying,*

Sophron: I found each of these talks revealed much about what concerns you. It gave me the opportunity to enter into the dilemma that you experience. It may not appear that what I will say about dreams may meet your profound needs, but I do think that it will do so because it opens a path that is no stranger to the divine.

For I speak as someone who has spent much time studying the world of dreams; they are man's gift from the divine. The world of dreams is the doorway into an intellectual and more rational world because it can introduce you to a profound way of learning about yourself that is providential. If I can make this clear it should provide you with a way to understand that there is a symmetry between the intelligible world and our everyday way of existing, which is to say between the spiritual realm and the mundane.

For what is illuminated through dreams is what is most appropriate to one's circumstances, so that each dreamer receives a particular good according to his or her immediate needs. To extend to all a good that is uniquely appropriate to each is to bestow on each what is providential to them. Surely, in filling intelligent beings with their goodness, the master of our dreams bestows upon all things that are capable of receiving it their particular good. It is for this reason that we can say that the Dream Master exercises providence towards all intelligent beings, for what she communicates is a good most appropriate for the dreamer's needs.

It is through the dream world that there is a return to one's source, to that place where reflections drawn from one's past and present are brought together for our benefit. Dreams are a profound source of guidance, and in our having to contemplate them they become our natural object of contemplation.

All intelligent beings are guided by this guiding knowledge. It is this knowledge that always benefits, and it is, in fact, the source of all knowledge. The only real and genuine knowledge is based upon and derived from dreams, since skills and crafts merely utilize the higher forms of knowledge for particular purposes. For it is through the reflection upon dreams that mankind has learned to use metaphors, similes, personifications, symbols, analogies and allegories.

The structure of the dream presents images metaphorically, and the states of mind experienced in the dream are treated as similes which brings an understanding of the mystery of the dream content. Clearly these are the tools necessary to express the deepest desires of man, and in communicating what he has learned through these tools he becomes and participates in the rational. The more we can enter into an understanding of this dream world, the more we can consciously join in our own development and nurture and become partners in our own evolution, and in this way we learn how the dream master communicates. Strangely enough, when we learn to understand this kind of communication we discover that there is no need to interpret dreams. For in finding our own book of meaning we gain confidence in our own intellectual ability and appreciate the need for understanding ourselves in our own terms.

The dream master's ability to select from each dreamer's own past what has been ignored and for the most part forgotten is a sign that the dream master has a profound understanding of each individual's life and destiny. The states of mind presented through the dream bear a likeness to a past scene in which one unknowingly concluded falsely about oneself and the reality confronting them. Being unaware that one carries these false conclusions into one's understanding of the present, one is trapped to repeat the past as if it were the present. The repetition of mistakes means that one has imposed upon the present a past pattern whose urgency obscures its irrational character. This unknowing superimposition of past beliefs upon the uniqueness of the present is the source of pathologos problems. It is by discovering how the dream relates to the everyday experiences of life that one is awakened to the dream's analogical structure. And unfolding the mystery of the dream's content analogically is to recognize a dream as an allegory for the soul's development into its own good.

As long as the particular language of the dreamer expresses false beliefs about the self, which we call a pathologos, there is always a block to the understanding. Once we reach an understanding of how the pathologos fetters and locks the soul's progress, there is a natural growth into the logos itself. For the images and relationships expressed in the dream mirror the soul's unknowing loyalty to one's false beliefs.

The dream master's ability to diagnosis and chart each dreamer's voyage shows the dream master's profound art of navigation and a knowledge of each of our storm-like struggles as we seek to become masters of our fate. Through each of our voyages we learn to become masters of ourselves and to navigate our uncertain seas. The mastery we gain here is for another journey, one that brings us along a sacred way that all our earlier hardships have prepared us for, one that brings us to the source and goal of all.

Thus, since an application of a knowledge for the benefit of the subject is called a profession or an art, we can conclude that the dream master possesses the highest art for the benefit of all who are capable of receiving and sharing in it.

The dream master then is our teacher and guide on a road that carries those who know through their life's journey. In the dawning realization that we are, indeed, a part of a caring universe we put aside the need for an unknowing belief in these things, and by that transition from belief to understanding we participate in a more wondrous caring universe. Now you can see why we say the dream master possesses an art, but it would be unfair to say all this without going on to say the rest. Yet to share this nobler part with you, I do not think I shall be able to sing worthily. Still it must be said if truth is to be our guide. You see this role of midwifery in personal problems, and even providing us with prophetic dreams and insights is only a small part of the dream master's art. It is the higher and the more profound we must speak of next.

To begin with, let me say that I am not a stranger to what I shall share with you. Indeed, I am fortunate to be able to say that I have verified within myself, through my own dream experience, all that I say. First then, the direct participation into that intelligible realm is of such a wondrous nature that once experienced all else is like a shadow compared with it. It has been said that we are very fortunate that we do not see such a thing with the human eye, for if we did it would arouse in us a truly terrible love, so great is its awe-inspiring numinous presence. The intelligible is Beauty; it is not different from mind. What is that but mind knowing itself in a divine radiance whose luminosity cannot be other than the most brilliant light of Being? It is because even this, the profoundest of all experiences, is open to us through dreams that the Dream Master can be said to have a divine source. For that which bestows upon us this wonder of wonders must itself be held in a higher honor than the gift bestowed. I wish to thank you for the opportunity to reflect with you and for your attentive listening.

Joseph: Harry got up just about as fast as Sophron sat down. Whatever reaction the audience had was cut short because just as Sophron's last words were said, Harry addressed the meeting. While Harry's talk appeared to be addressed to all it was obvious from the start that the brunt of it was directed at Sophron. Harry was like that and as impatient and impulsive as a really hungry man might be before a banquet table. He started abruptly.

Harry: So metaphysics is coming out of the closet and we are expected to invite her to sit down at the head of the table, the place of honor and authority. But don't let her sit down among us until we recall why she has had to hide. Let me recall something I've learned more than once and that is that the whole European development of thought that brought us so much progress has been called for good reason the Age of Enlightenment.

This movement of thought brought Rationalism into the open, discoveries were made in every area open to the sciences, and chief among these advances was the stability it brought to our government and institutions. Those that framed this development made sure everyone knew that the primary obstacle to their success was metaphysics. To expend one's energies on what is beyond the reach of any mind is to utterly waste one's resources on the impossible. I woke up from my own delusions through David Hume and what he said is indelibly etched in my brain. He said, "The ultimate springs and principles are totally shut up from human curiosity and inquiry."

We need to be clear about why this kind of thinking is returning. It is not because metaphysics is being rediscovered, as if there is a need for us to return to flights of fancy. All this recent talk among cosmologists, physicists, and mathematicians has made respectable issues that were once thought of as metaphysical. All you need to do is pick up any modern book since Hawking's work of time and you'll find that these people are taking off from their research findings; they are speculating on the implications of their findings, but that's not metaphysics because metaphysics has no such foundations. The issues they talk about, such as the origin of the universe, determinism, the collapse of the universe, and the God particle all sound metaphysical, but they should be called meta-scientific not metaphysical. Philosophy is riding on the coattails of science in using scientific categories, its models, and its major theoretical concepts. It makes believe it should take an honored chair here at our banquet.

Let me ask your members here in the audience if they ever heard or read of any philosopher ever talking about this idea of symmetry before our scientific community discovered its importance. Go ahead, who can say they recall any philosopher talking about the importance of symmetry? See? There are no hands up, not even one.

Here we have philosophy making believe it is on the par with science as it talks about symmetry, but we know that this idea was developed through the sciences after many arduous years of effort and struggle. Don't get me wrong; I am not saying I don't understand all the fine words Sophron has just said—far from it. No matter how fine you put these words together, you have to acknowledge that the words are not yours. Sure, his words sound great because they are arranged together and presented as if they really harmonize together. But that's only because this maestro here is a good composer of lyrics. Sure you can paint a castle of your dreams on the wall of your hut, but that doesn't mean you can move into one of its stately rooms.

I'll tell you the problem with all this interpretation of dreams, and it's real simple. It works, and that's the problem. I do not doubt for a single moment that there are people like Sophron who are excellent at interpreting dreams. It's a fact. Why argue it? I'm sure that there are other equally talented people who can do the same thing even from different schools of thought. Each of them may indeed represent this or that school of dream interpretation and with equal skill convey to the dreamer the richness they perceive in the dreams they analyze. Here is the point: it is not that the system is intelligible, it's the way certain people can intuit the dream, pour it into their own interpretative system, and communicate it to the dreamer. That is the point. These people could do the same thing reading tarot cards, tea leaves, the *I Ching*, or what not. No dream analyst can justify their system by pointing to their success, because it is not repeatable, and that means if you teach it to just anyone you won't get the same results; that's all there is to it. It is for this reason that I'm not interested in Sophron's dream interpretation or his theories. In truth, they don't know why their system works; they can't explain what they are doing as they proceed through their dream analysis.

Now, don't misunderstand me. I am not saying that he won't do a good job and astonish this audience with his skill. It is just that it is irrelevant to the point. I'll make it simpler. You can't prove there is any rationality in man's experience by any interpretative system because all you are doing is proving the system works when some intuitive genius uses it. Now, the same thing is true for psychotherapy and any counseling method; none of them can be used to prove man's rationality since the system they use is like a sieve or a trap that catches what they need for analysis. It's the sieve we should look at for rationality, not the man.

So what? I'll tell you what. Prove to me that you can take a present difficulty someone is having and explore it to see if there is any rationality behind it. Don't use some well defined and structured statement of a problem that already has the material implanted for analysis. The patient walks into the therapist's office and knows what to say to get the therapist to help them. It's not the system, it's giving that kind of intuitive person the entrails to divine your future. No way; rather take a non-problem; take a simple random kind of human experience that someone is having that bugs them. Don't go for anxiety, depressions, or any traumatic event; just take something we all can see as a case of spilled milk, do you know what I mean? These everyday events are what bug us all, so just make sense of those kinds of things. Present it for review, and tell us as you go along what you are doing to find the rationality behind it. And then, and only then, talk about rationality and meaning, but not before.

Now, let me tell you that my friend here, Julie, has told me she couldn't sleep much last night because of a back pain. I'm not in charge here, I'm just offering a suggestion. Sophron, why not explore this in any way that you want and see if you can make any sense of it other than saying she has a back pain because she feels a pain in her back? Take that as something to explore and show us there is something going on behind the scenes that even suggests that we are part of some rational and caring universe.

You may not want to explore it here in front of all these people, or you might take the challenge, I don't know which you'll do. Some people here may have heard enough of this session and would like to leave. However, if we are really serious here and want to test the limits of theory and practice, I say let's see one at work. So let's take a break, let Sophron decide how he wants to proceed, and for those who want to see how the challenge unfolds, let's stick around and see what develops.

> **Joseph:** *Sophron got up just about as fast as Harry went to sit down. He slipped into high gear as quickly as Harry had done previously. It was kind of fun to watch. The tables were turned on Harry and now it was Sophron who caught the audiences' attention. He turned to Harry and in a disarming sort of way replied.*

Sophron: Actually, you are correct, in a certain way, Harry, since you are bringing up the fundamental problem of our age: the nature and use of interpretation within systems. It is a curious problem that needs our attention. Consider, what condition must the original work be in if it needs to be interpreted? The degree to which a work needs to be interpreted, to that very degree the work itself is weak and needs something outside itself to support it. For surely if it needs to be added to or if parts should be ignored then in modifying the work in this way the interpreter transforms the work to represent another viewpoint that was not contained in the original work. For to interpret means to add, subtract, or modify some material so that it expresses the interpreter's own viewpoint. In going beyond the work the interpreter needs to appear as sincere and possessing more insight and knowledge than what was formerly believed true.

The believer must have been convinced that the interpreter knew what should have been seen before the interpretation, or there would be no reason to believe the interpretation. Thus, the act of believing is at the same time the moment of sacrificing one's own understanding. It is this forfeiting of one's own understanding that allows an authority to be placed over oneself; and when that authority's interpretation cannot be questioned, tyranny is born. This process is part of the art of rhetoric and is akin to the creating of illusion, or magic. It is certainly important to understand this issue. I would like to offer a demonstration workshop based upon this game of interpretation in order to show the dynamics for inculcating belief, but for now we must return to the other issues that you raised.

If she wishes I will gladly explore this difficulty that your friend has reported, but as for its outcome, neither I nor you can predict it. Is there something to pain, to a sleepless night, or being late, and such things? Is there a moment without meaning? Is it at all possible that there are no chance elements in our existence? Are there events without meaning, such as accidents? Is meaning the symmetry between everyday events and the intelligible? And, if there is, can we discover it? Very nice questions.

Joseph: *Some people left, and others rearranged their chairs and sitting cushions in anticipation of the talk. Sophron turned and spoke to Julie and as he did, he shook her hand warmly and thanked her for allowing him to discuss her difficulty in public.*

THE SYMMETRY, PART 3:
SOPHRON AND JULIE WITH OTHERS[1]

Joseph: *After a short time the session was ready to resume. Sophron and Julie were talking together. She spoke about her difficulty sleeping and her experience of pain. Sophron was sketching out her remarks on the flip-chart. The drawings were simple. He took care to accurately write out certain things that she said. She had a recorder sitting on the table. He asked her to repeat certain parts and said that if she recalled anything else that she may have forgotten, to add it to her account. This made the talk even more interesting because now everyone could reflect on her story as it was sketched out on the flip-chart and see how the analysis progressed. Helen told me, "Our concern shifted from Julie to trying to carefully follow what was on the flip charts. In that way Sophron made her mystery ours, and it became the center of all our concern." Sophron turned to the group and reviewed with us his own reflections.*

Sophron: *Consider what we know: She had a back pain, and was not able to sleep. We may not get anywhere with it, but it should help us put limitations on our explorations.*[2] Isn't that nice to know?

Julie: Yes.

Sophron: Notice that the first question is the most difficult one to answer in our midwifery which is, "What is your problem?"

Julie: But I don't know what the problem is.

Sophron: *That's right. She doesn't even know whether it is a problem. That's why we are doing it.*

Julie: But I did experience a certain amount of suffering that seemed unnecessary, it seemed like I prolonged it or resisted doing anything about it, or thought that I was helpless. I kept trying to massage my own back because I have a knot right here under my shoulder blade that really– that's chronic. I have had it for many years; it occasionally flares up and it gets so tight and so painful that it goes right up to this side of my

---

[1] This talk was a dialogue that took place during a workshop at the Church of Religious Science in Carson City Nevada. The transcript was made by Julie Grabel and edited by Pierre Grimes. Every effort was made to keep the editing as close as possible to the actual talk.

[2] Sophron's remarks directed to everyone present are in italics as a means to distinguish those from his remarks and questions in the direct dialogue with Julie.

head and gives me a headache on my right side. And sometimes I get people to rub my back; sometimes I tried to rub my own back, but no matter what I did I just couldn't break through it. And I got frustrated by that, tossed and turned, realized that I hadn't brought any Tylenol with me, but never even considered getting up and getting dressed and going out to the casino to buy some Tylenol; I just stayed in bed tossing and turning all night long until my wake-up call came and it was time to get up and take a shower. So I don't know if that's a problem, but it seems like there might be some kind of emotional or psychological holding going on that's being concentrated in that area.

Sophron: Uh, yes.

Julie: It would be wonderful if I could get rid of a condition that I've had for a long time. If it were related in some way to my state of mind, now that would be fascinating.

Sophron: *There is no point in exploring pain, so I am going to explore the state of mind she was in, tossing in bed. So I will talk about it, and then we will explore it. There are several things that are significant in the talk. One is that in the past she would get people to rub her back, and this time she did it to herself and wasn't able to relieve it, tossed and turned. An apparent solution or remedy was not available, no Tylenol. Then, she reflected on being in bed. She recognized that she had a solution and didn't draw upon it, which was to go out and get some Tylenol, so therefore she stayed in that condition and tossed.* Now, what was it like being in bed? You stayed and tossed, didn't go to get your Tylenol.

Julie: I didn't even consider going out, that is the thing. I didn't even think of it.

Sophron: Then, what thoughts and reflections did you have? Because in forgetting one forgets the solution, so now what goes on when you stay in your state? What is it like?

Julie: I tried to handle it myself. I tried to find the place in my back with my left arm—reaching over trying to find it—but it is just out of reach. I can't quite penetrate deep enough into it with my own hand. It is just out of reach, so I would say things like, "Oh come on!" or "Oh, please!"

Sophron: Please continue.

Julie: So, I tried different positions, lay on my back for awhile; then the pain in my head would start throbbing, and I would put my finger on that pressure point and try a little acupressure, and that relieved it somewhat. It was a constant thing: if I wasn't doing something to the pain, to like counter it, it would be bothering me. And so the pain would stop a little bit while I was working on it, but I couldn't sleep. I couldn't sleep while I was doing that, so–

Sophron: What is it like doing that, please? There you are trying to find pressure points, "can't penetrate it," searching for the physical source of it. You're going through all of that, aren't you? *Now, please note that in midwifery it is good to recollect what the person has said just as we are doing now, this allows reflection to bring the terms back.* So, you can't find the pressure points, can't find the physical.

Julie: You know, what comes to mind, it is a narrowing. It is like my focus is very narrow at that time, like I'm not— I kind of pull within and it is real narrow, like there is–

Sophron: What?

Julie: Like tunnel vision, very narrow, and it is like I don't have access to it. It is like that forgetfulness; I don't have access to anything outside of that tiny little area.

Sophron: And what is that like? *Note again that one should always ask for similes, always similes when you need a description of states of mind.*

Julie: It is restrictive, it is restricting.

Sophron: I don't know what that means.

Julie: Limited.

Sophron: Say, if you're in a state that for you is limiting and restrictive, narrow, focusing, what is that like? It is like being? Go ahead.

Julie: Trapped came to mind.

Sophron: Trapped. Go ahead, trapped, as if what? Expand the simile, expand the simile. So, trapped as if what?

Julie: I don't know– Held down.

Sophron: Held down.

Julie: I can feel the physical sensation of holding my breath and like that, holding my breath and clenching my fists.

Sophron: You say, "I can't penetrate it, it is like out of my reach, I'm looking for pressure points. I just can't do it. Looking for the physical, trying to reach it myself..." Recall that you gave that interesting expression before. Come on. Please recall what you described a moment ago. You said it was a kind of tunneling, narrow focus, it is restricting and limiting, it is like being trapped, like you're held down, holding your breath, fists are clenched; for that is an interesting state of mind. *Please notice that there is a certain kind of language here that in some sense may be parallel to the physical symptoms. But you just note that, you don't say anything about it, file it away. It may not turn out to be important. What we try to do is to get the vocabulary from the subject. So you've got to hold yourself back from interpreting.*

Julie: I think that when you're trapped and held down, you're not in control; somebody else is or something else is.

Sophron: Yeah, notice how the role of forgetfulness plays itself out?

Julie: It is even worse than forgetfulness; it's like obstinacy to me.

Helen: That is a good word.

Julie: It is like– Damn! Like why would I stay there all night like that when I could do something about it so quickly, so easily. I know Tylenol isn't the cure, but it certainly helps the symptoms enough to allow me to go to sleep. I'm very sensitive to medication, it doesn't take much. The idea to get Tylenol seems like it kind of started to come in and I like *pshhh*.

Sophron: The word obstinate: What does that mean to you?

Julie: Stubborn.

Sophron: Stubborn.

Julie: Like resistant to do anything about it to the point where I'm wondering, did I want to cultivate it? Like, was this–

Sophron: Stubborn and obstinate?

Julie: People are usually stubborn and obstinate when they have an idea and they want to push that idea. Here I am in pain; and it is like I'm obstinate about getting rid of it; I mean it is like a negative thing.

Sophron: What is that like, this obstinate and stubborn stuff? What is that like? *Please note that I'm going now for another state of mind, see?* What is it like being stubborn, obstinate? *I'm asking because a moment ago she described it negatively. Don't take negative explanations or descriptions for states of mind.*

Helen: So you don't want to know what it is not like?

Sophron: *Yes, famous statement about an elephant, if you describe all the ways it is not, what do you have? For it tells you nothing about what an elephant is.* Say, but I don't understand obstinate, stubborn. What is that like, again? It is as if what?

Julie: It is funny because I can do it.

Sophron: Well, do it and well–

Julie: I see it; it is like I see it.

Sophron: Really?

Julie: I see it as a gesture, as a body gesture, as a way of, like preventing myself from seeing something, like, don't go there. It is like that right now. I feel like I'm doing it right now. I'm not able to get in touch with what it is like. It is like a little voice is doing it right now to my head. Don't do it, don't go there, like this resistance, there is something holding me back.

Sophron: *Please note that forgetfulness, no it is not forgetfulness, there is something in addition, there is a certain obstinate state that is in there. It is not obstinate, it is kind of a stubborn, no, it is not quite a stubborn.* Describe what it is like.

Julie: Disregarding, too.

Sophron: Don't go there, don't do it, disregard—go ahead.

Julie: The thought comes in ever so quickly and before it can even get to the conscious level where I would have to deal with it, I'm pushing it away.

Sophron: *Again, please note that it is always good to go from this kind of language—obstinate, stubborn—to a language which describes a physical and emotional action as with "push it away," right? That follows the word, see "disregard" doesn't have an image. Always go for the image behind the language because that is the way the mind thinks.* So, that is what we were doing, see, we landed a rich image. "Don't go there, don't do that, push it away." That describes an interesting state, doesn't it? Notice, too, that the language also stresses "don'ts." Are those statements like a commandment?

Julie: Yes.

Sophron: *Always look for that. Those are the principles upon which a certain behavior depends. When you hear it, note it.* Say, it is likely you're familiar with that state, are you not? Disregard it, don't go there,

The Symmetry, Part 3

push it away, don't do that, stubborn, obstinate

Julie: Hmm hmm

Sophron: At what age would you say you can come up with something that's similar to that? Last year, ten years, anything at all?

Julie: I don't know, I was just noticing that it also happened in the ears.

Sophron: Ears?

Julie: There is a closing down. Like, I can tell when it happens in dialogue, too—when I've entered that state and I can feel that I'm not able to listen.

Sophron: *Now notice, we have two states of mind, all right? Notice how they emerged. There is one state of mind that keeps and allows the other. Without this forgetfulness she would use her solution.* Get some Tylenol, right?

Julie: It is as if I don't want the pain to go away. It is as if it's there for a purpose. I feel like playing it out or something. And yet I was going: "Oh my God, I need some sleep," and "Please, I want some sleep!" Like, I'm going to be a mess if I don't get some sleep.

Sophron: But the idea of forgetfulness is not accurate enough. It is actually a closing down, see? *Note, the forgetfulness allows this struggle to emerge so that we could identity this. Notice the difference between these two: forgetfulness– No image, and closing down– Image! Ahhh..*

Julie: Now, that reminds me of a past scene I have recalled.

Sophron: How old?

Julie: The closing down. See, it's probably– I think I'm like nine or ten.

Sophron: *Now, notice. We're not doing anything with the recollection for a moment.* Say, when you were in that state that you closed down narrow, tunnel-like, remember, restricting limited, but that turned out to be trapped, held down, right? Images, metaphors. Held down, expression. Physiological, holding the breath, clenching the fists.

Julie: Oh that is fascinating 'cause I just saw now that that is in the same scene! Ah! From the other side. Oh my goodness!

Sophron: Now, before you go ahead, there is something curious about this. Let's go back to that theme because it looks like there may be something else there.

Julie: Can I tell you that already the pain in my back has lessened. Wow!

Sophron: *We're going to do the same thing as we did before, aren't we?* Good. Say, I'm not sure I understand what you mean when you said, "You can't penetrate it; it is like out of reach." Talk about that. Say, what is that like, I don't understand it. Talk about "can't penetrate, out of reach." Put more words on that. Describe it better.

Julie: I can describe it. I don't know if I can see what it is like, but it is–

Sophron: Well, before you say what it is like, just talk about it for a moment, and then we can see what it is like after.

Julie: See, I can put my mind on it. I can reach it in my mind and I feel like I should be able to put my finger right on it, and when I try to do that and I push as hard as I can, I just cannot penetrate it. It just won't– It is not able to penetrate what my mind can see. So I try a meditation where I actually look at it with mind and ask myself what is aware of it in an attempt to break it, sometimes it works, but–

Sophron: Put a couple more words on it, "Can't reach, can't put my finger on it, can't penetrate it, not able to see."

Julie: Intense concentration as I try to do it, focus. But a frustration at not being able to accomplish it. Anguish, more anguish than frustration.

David: Sophron, can I ask you? You shook your head and said no to frustration and then you wrote down anguish. What was the reason?

Sophron: Obstinate? I won't accept it. Frustration? I won't accept it. There is no image behind those words. What does that mean? That means the person didn't choose that word to capture some state that they're in. It is popular psychological language. See, we have a language that comes to us from several different traditions and languages. All Latin roots have no images unless you know the Latin.

Julie: Has no image?

Sophron: *Has no images for us. The languages that preserve their roots, cultures that keep alive the roots of their language always have an edge on reflection because the images are still alive. When you import language that has no image then you're literally in the realm of abstraction that is remote from all experience. We are trying to reach a level of reflection that can more accurately describe our experience. It is by searching for words that can vivify and enrich past memories that we find the keys to understand these past scenes. In this way, the possible parallels and similarities of both the past and its analogous situ-*

ations become available for exploration and comparison.

Now let's look at the idea of frustration. What is it? What's the difference between frustration and closing down? See, the word frustration allows such a wide range of meaning that it's not usable, though you know it is some kind of distress, that's clear. We want to get away from that range of uses so that you can find something that is expressive of a person's unique experience. Therefore, you avoid Latin-rooted words and psychological terms to get closer to the person's way of experience, find their private language. If the origin of the pathologos, false beliefs about oneself, are framed in the child's language it is likely to reflect a language free from complex abstractions. Why? Because it reflects the most immediate experience they have and they're trying to desperately put words on it, they're trying to find simple old words to bring it together, and that's the struggle to understand.

David: So, the word anguish is less broad.

Sophron: *Please consider this thought. We can grasp the meaning behind all kinds of images. I'm not satisfied until the words reveal a specific particularity, or the specificity of one's experience. The more a person describes this experience in personal terms, the richer is their reflection and the closer they are able to reach meaning. And meaning is never on the surface, it is something that is behind it and is that which is responsible for the forms.*

Now, Julie, you say you can't penetrate, are not able to perceive (reach) it, but in some way your mind can see and you're trying to focus your mind to see something that's just outside of your reach, you can't put your finger on it. It builds up an intense concentration, doesn't it?

Again, note that when you are satisfied with a description of the state of mind that's behind the key words, then you can say what that is like, that's a simile. You can't get any precision in a simile that is too broad. It'll go too many places.

That's interesting. Say, that is interesting. Go over it for me, will you? Recall your remark, "Can't put your finger on it, can't quite reach it."

Julie: Can't dig in deep enough.

Sophron: Go ahead.

Julie: That's really what it is, I can't dig in deep enough.

Sophron: "Can't get deep enough, blocked in getting deep."

Julie: Yeah, I feel that it is just out of my reach, that I can't get to it, I can't push hard enough.

Sophron: You say, "You can't get deep enough—blocked in getting deep," What is that like? *Simile now*. What is that like?

Julie: Well, I have the image of reaching and being able to see something just beyond my grasp.

Sophron: Yes.

Julie: Whatever that is that is beyond my grasp is also– I don't want to say that it is pulled away from me as I get closer to it, but it has that fading, it has that image to me of fading so that it is not clear, somehow muffled or clouded. That lack of clarity has something to do with why I can't reach it, too.

Sophron: Yeah, now for a moment think about it, OK? *When a person is engaged in a dialogue like this and they suggest something and chop it off, you go back to it, just to give them a chance to try it again.* Do you remember what she said and what she chopped off? Fake, you went from fake to fading, you chopped off the word fake.

Julie: I didn't say fake.

Sophron: Play it back.

Julie: Really?

Sophron: Play it back *[They play it back and hear the word "fake." It is said so quickly they can hardly hear it, but it is there.]*

Julie: Now, this reminds me of dreams, because that's one of the valuable things about my dreams since you'll get a word like that and it'll surprise you, and they always surprise me that I don't know where those words come from. But if you get it on the tape and you transcribe it, you use it—you don't try to change it.

Sophron: It is something you're after, "It's just out of your reach. It's fading, it's not clear, it is as if someone is taking it away." Right? It is a motion. *Just keep that idea of fake in the background, interesting.*

Julie: I don't know if that's right.

Sophron: *Again note that what is nice about this game is that you don't have to be right. Just keep open all the possibilities, but it is a curious word that nearly came out. Maybe someone did a bait and switch game on her. It would be difficult at first to accept that as something that is going on, so I would back away from that conclusion and say, "Oh the object faded away, the object became clouded." It may be that you're blaming the object, not the person. Fake suggests duplicity, an agent.*

Julie: I don't have any feeling that there is anything on the other side of the thing that I'm trying to reach for that could be pulling it in and out. I don't have that.

Sophron: *Consider for a moment what went on. When I heard that word, I said, "Interesting." There is an agent. So what do you do? You put it aside. Make a little note, file it, don't lose it.* Now again, what is this like? If you had to find a situation where that might be, what might that be like?

Julie: It is like looking for the right word when I'm talking, like having the idea that I can express something but I don't. I can't find the right word. Like you think it almost comes into your mind, but then it darts away so fast that you can't catch it.

Sophron: That's what we get when we explore that idea.

Julie: That's great, I had no idea.

Sophron: So, we have three states of mind now, don't we? One, two, three.

Julie: And you know what, too? This happened yesterday. It is like thinking that I understand something and I want to express it to someone and as soon as I try to put words on it, they aren't there. I can't find the right words to express what it is I saw or thought I saw, which in my experience usually means I didn't understand it well enough. I didn't understand it as well as I thought I did.

Sophron: *Make the search for the words the object of curiosity, not the person, because it is what the individual is saying and searching for that is important. The person you are talking to, the subject, is struggling to achieve understanding with the material they present. This is the material on the board. This is, as it were, trying to come up with a painting and these are the strokes and these are the colors you are using and the artist is trying to find the thing that they are trying to bring into existence, so you can look at the canvas, the mystery is in the canvas. So you want to make sure that everything that's there has the integrity of the dreamer, the integrity of the person, the integrity to the problem; so you use their language, their images, their expressions.*

David: It could easily become a debate about interpretations except you're avoiding all that. You're both sitting on the same log looking out at this, yeah, and that makes you a team working on it, and you're not opposing each other in any way, you're both supporting each other.

Sophron: *[reflecting] Now join me as I look over our notes on the flip chart. Let's see whether there might not be some other thing to explore. We might find another state of mind. At this point it doesn't appear I can see any. But when we explore a past experience, we may go back here and see there are things we have overlooked.* So what happened? What is the thing that you remembered that you recalled a moment ago?

Julie: This scene has both of those states of mind. That's great that it has both of those! I was about nine. We had a garage in the back of our house. It was a separate building and it had an upstairs to it that you could get to by climbing up a ladder that was flush with the wall in the back of the garage, and you could climb up this ladder and get to the top and it was not, according to my parents, not a safe place to be. The floorboards were supposedly weak but I never saw any evidence of that. But there was old furniture up there and a perfectly delightful place for a child to go to be alone, to play or to be somewhere where nobody could find me.

One particular day I went up there and my brother was up there. My brother is three years older than I am. And he took this opportunity to push me down on the couch and jump on top of me, and he was holding me down, and I was very scared and uncomfortable and telling him to stop and he was– He was enjoying my discomfort. At least that is the way I look at it now. I look back at it, and he got a charge out of it: the more I would resist, the more he would pressure me. I don't remember him actually– I don't remember it actually being sexual, but I knew that there was something sexual about it; I'm not sure how or why I knew that.

It almost seems as if it wasn't the first time, it wasn't the first time that this kind of thing had happened because of the— Because when I went in to tell my mother about it— I broke away and went in the house and I found my mother and I tried to tell her what my brother Chip had done, you know, "Mom, Chipper just trapped me up in the garage and wouldn't let me go and was– He jumped on top of me, and it was horrible!" And I'm crying. And, her reaction is to chuckle and to tell me, "Oh Julie, you're exaggerating. I'm sure it was nothing. He didn't mean anything by it and you shouldn't be up there anyway." And she waved me off, disregarded me, and wouldn't let me talk about it anymore, didn't want to hear it, didn't want to hear it. Like I was inconveniencing her now. "Don't bother me." That is it. I don't remember what happened after that, I don't know, I walked away from that shaking my head, probably like this *[shaking head, no]* Boy, are we going to get the head shaking, too? Oh my goodness gracious, two or three for the price of one, this'll be great.

Sophron: *As you go back into the states of mind, clearly you see certain parallels, right? And what we do is say and raise this question and this is where, this is the key part now, OK? We want to see whether we can get the person to understand this. We want to see whether or not the words capture the conclusions that are drawn from this scene. Did the mother help her conclude? No. Therefore the subject has to walk away and try to understand what went on. This is the very nature of our task because we don't know the conclusions that she reached, nor does she, yet the conclusions have a continuous impact on the psyche. So, how do you proceed? Which do you think is having the greater impact? The event itself or trying to understand the total event which, of course, includes the mother's participation. You really have two events, you see. You have this event upstairs in the garage, and you have this interrelationship between the mother and the daughter. The event never produces a problem. It is the conclusions you draw from it that are not expressed, and that is why it keeps coming up. See, the mind keeps giving you, again and again in a variety of ways, these inappropriate conclusions, which means the mind doesn't like to have false beliefs about its own experience.*

Julie: You know, what is interesting is that as I sit here and let this trickle in, I think part of what I concluded I didn't describe properly; I didn't say what I should have said– Like something that I could have said would have made her see that it was real. I didn't do something right.

Sophron: So, "It's my fault! I didn't express it. Had I, she would have been able to deal with it." Keep going.

Julie: Right. That is because, that is it. It is like what did I do wrong? Why didn't she see what I was trying to tell her? Come on! It was so obvious. It caught me off guard that she didn't believe me. It was like– I felt like she didn't believe me, that nothing had happened and that I was just being overly dramatic about something that didn't have any significance, and yet, you know, here I was: I felt that it was real and yet I wasn't able to communicate that to her so therefore–

Sophron: *Now, in order to raise the level of this reflection, you need as much detail as you can get. Start a puzzle, develop a puzzle so you go back to the statements and see whether you can reconcile them with the event. So, I will pick one, all right?* That is pretty interesting, Julie. By the way, what does it mean for her to say that he didn't mean anything. What does that mean?

Julie: It means that she thought I was overreacting.

Sophron: Pardon me. Is she describing you or is she describing what she is doing?

Julie: See, it is as if she wants to say she knows him so well that she can tell by my description that he didn't mean anything by it. Maybe it was because I didn't tell her that he took his clothes off or something like that. The fact that he didn't take his clothes off means that it wasn't sexual; therefore, it wasn't serious; therefore, he didn't mean anything by it. It was all in good fun, like every older brother does this to their younger sisters, like you shouldn't take it seriously; it doesn't mean anything.

Sophron: W*ould you agree we were dealing with the theme "I didn't express it right, I didn't describe what went on." Now, I've picked one phrase and focused on it and want to know whether or not it fits the scene. That is what we're doing.* Say, did you say, "I didn't express it right, therefore mother didn't…" go ahead, finish it.

Julie: She didn't understand.

Sophron: Hold it, for just one moment. Hear it? OK, go ahead. "It is my fault, I didn't express it right," so she didn't know what was going on. Go ahead.

Julie: I don't know how she could possibly know he didn't mean anything by it.

Sophron: But does that deny it happened?

Julie: That is the way I felt about it.

Sophron: I know, I just wondered about the words, just the words.

Julie: He didn't mean anything by it.

Sophron: Does that mean she doesn't understand what went on?

Julie: I guess it means that even if she did understand what went on, she is concluding that it didn't mean anything.

Sophron: Is she denying the event. No, she is denying the significance of it. So you're trying to describe and express the event as if she's having trouble understanding what went on.

Julie: See, it doesn't matter what went on; what she should have dealt with was what I was feeling.

Sophron: Thank you.

Julie: It doesn't matter whether he was really raping me or it just felt like it to me. I would have thought now as an adult, if I look back at a scene like this, if someone has an experience like that, don't you want to deal with what they perceive or how they feel about it?

Sophron: That may be true...

Julie: She wasn't dealing with me at all.

Sophron: Yes. What we want to see though is just her words and what those words mean. And what you're saying is quite proper. We're just looking at these words, "I'm sure it was nothing." I'm picking the next one. Does that mean she's denying that it went on?

Julie: No.

Sophron: Are you trying to express it in such a way that she can understand what went on? Is she denying what went on?

Julie: That is what I thought.

Sophron: I just wondered about the words.

Julie: I don't know exactly what to focus on to answer your question. Like, "He didn't mean anything," is as if she knows him so well that she can say that what I described was no big deal.

Sophron: Let's go back over it. Would you agree, when you walked away, as it were, from the scene, you're blaming yourself for something. "I didn't express it properly. Had I expressed it properly she would have understood what was going on." This is your conclusion.

Julie: I'm also thinking that she's telling me that I shouldn't react the way I'm reacting.

Sophron: That certainly is there, but is your conclusion proper? Is it that you didn't express it correctly so she didn't picture what was going on?

Julie: I guess not. I guess I expressed it. I guess she's reacting to what I said.

Sophron: "I'm sure it was nothing." Is it denying the event took place?

Julie: She's saying that no matter what happened, it didn't mean anything, that it wasn't significant.

Sophron: Oh, if that is true, then what are you trying to do? You're blaming yourself for doing something that you need to do or don't need to do? Heh. You know what was wrong with that scene? Do you know what happened? "I didn't express it right, I didn't put the right words on it, the words are just out of my reach, I couldn't get the right words to express, cause if I only expressed it right then she'd know what was going on." And you conclude, "That was my problem, that is why she reacted the way she did."

Julie: Yeah, because otherwise I can't make any sense out of why she would negate, wipe out, disregard what I'm saying.

Sophron: Good. That is right.

Julie: Either I have to think she is being unjust, or I have to think I screwed up.

Sophron: That is right. Now, we got it.

Steve: That articulates so well with the don't go there, push it away, disregard it.

Sophron: Yes, right.

Julie: That is the story of my mom, that is my life with her.

Sophron: When we're caught–

Julie: Because if she takes what I say for real then she has to deal with Chip; she has to deal with it, and she doesn't want to and that is her mantra: "Don't go there, don't push it, don't do it, don't go there".

Sophron: As a child of nine, what would it be like to live knowing that about your mother? That you could be in a scene that might be a scene where you might be violated in this way and how will she relate to it?

OK, and now how are you going to live with that? Oh, she's my protector, right; she's the one who really–

Julie: No.

Sophron: So, what are you going to do? You have the two alternatives. You're going to take this one, aren't you? "I failed to express it."

Harry: Does lack of acknowledgment always result in self blame?

Sophron: Yes.

Steve: The particular significance of this scene is that it happened in her safe place.

Sophron: Yes.

Julie: I loved that place, I hated it when they took it away. They boarded it up, and I couldn't go up there anymore.

Sophron: After this, they boarded it up? Oh, well, then nothing took place!

Steve: Not only didn't it happen, but you can't even go there.

Sophron: Nothing happened! But is that right? He would never do that. But the place was boarded up.

Julie: I never even thought about that until just now, but I think it was shortly after that that they made it impossible for me to get up there.

Grace: You said that mind does not like to believe. What do you mean?

Sophron: There is something about concluding falsely. Did she conclude falsely, first of all? The problem I had from that scene is this: "It is my fault; I wasn't able to express what went on with sufficient clarity so my mother then would be able to understand what went on and deal with it intelligently."

Julie: The person who is supposed to love you and protect you is not able to, not going to be there for you. The mind doesn't want to accept that.

Sophron: Yes, that is particular. Grace raised the question in general which is, what is it about that particular conclusion that is offensive to the mind? It will not accept you accepting the blame for something when it is someone else's responsibility and not your problem.

Grace: Therefore it continued on as a problem.

Julie: Bugging me, that is right, it is still bugging me.

Sophron: Watch now. We will take one more step and then I think we'll have it. Say, when you walked away with that conclusion, that was your... what would you call it, something you failed?

Julie: I didn't say it right or didn't describe it properly, or—

Sophron: See, isn't that a failure on your part, something you can't do?

Julie: I failed to communicate.

Sophron: Is this what you are saying, "You can't do something, it is your failure, you can't communicate" because all of these I can't, I can't, I can't, they come together in an image of the self as someone who can't be relied upon to... what? Will you put aside these "I can't" words and pick up these colors and draw a picture of the image you have of yourself as you walked away from that scene. Go ahead. Here is some colored chalk.

Julie: I can't draw.

Sophron: You don't want me to do it, do you?

Julie: Yes, I do.

Sophron: Oh, well then direct me. Go ahead.

Julie: I have this image of somebody kind of hunched over with my head down.

Sophron: Go ahead. Go ahead.

Julie: Yes

Sophron: Go ahead, with what look on the face?

Julie: Sad, but you know what is funny is that I have this image that it wasn't too long after I turned around and walked away that the whole thing just vanished. I mean, I don't even have any sense that I thought about it for very long after that.

Sophron: Yeah, of course not.

Julie: That it was just gone.

Sophron: Yeah! It is all gone. Forgetfulness. It is gone.

Julie: It is gone, I mean I was gone, I was out of there.

Sophron: *Maybe this image that she concluded about herself stays. Every problem exists solely because one has a false image of the self. The mind refuses to accept a false image of itself. Therefore, it is going to put that in front of you anytime you want to achieve something where that image is inconsistent with your goal. It has this kind of logic. If you dare think and believe I am this, then if you want to struggle for*

The Symmetry, Part 3
49

some goal, you're going to have to change the image of yourself. You're going to have to give up that false image to get it. That is all there is to it.

David: So this fits in nicely for me. It was the Tylenol.

Julie: Because?

David: Well, what you didn't want to do was you didn't want to take the Tylenol and make the situation go away like it did here. Notice you took the Tylenol by concluding about yourself that you were at fault instead of what you knew was at fault, but you couldn't accept that. So you resolved the tension in this situation; you took the Tylenol to make it go away, make the pain go away. It was gone, the headache, as soon as you decided it was your fault. So, *here* in this recapitulation now, the problem is still with you, and it hasn't been resolved. You're getting tired of it. So, "by God, I'm not taking the Tylenol this time!"

Julie: I see what you mean. It is funny, 'cause it is escalating.

Sophron: Courage. There is a new courage coming into the picture.

Julie: See, I want to see what the hell is going on here!

Sophron: See, that is courage.

David: You refused to take the Tylenol.

Sophron: You need to keep your cool and have courage. Can't do the game without keeping your cool, right? Facing it—that takes courage. And you have to be fair, absolutely fair, right? You have to be fair to the scenes in the past, you have to express it as accurately as you can. You can't lay the blame on anybody. You have to take a look at it, every part has to be where it is, just where it is. And do you know what that is?

Julie: Justice?

Sophron: That is justice, and you want to express it with such clarity that you know your judgments are sound. You want to be sure your judgments are sound. You know what these are?

Julie: Virtues?

Sophron: These are the four cardinal virtues. Keeping your cool is level-headedness. Keeping a sound mind. We call it keeping your cool. The classic word for it is temperance. Temperance, *sofrosune,* the Greek word, literally means sound mind. Keep your cool, right? Don't blow up, keep your cool, man. It takes courage to play this game, doesn't it? To face yourself, face your past, try to come to terms with it? You have to be fair. Justice. Your judgments have to be sound, they have to reflect a reality. That is a kind of wisdom, isn't it? These are the four cardinal virtues, and philosophical midwifery cannot exist and cannot function without their presence. The presence of these allows us to look directly at these scenes with greater integrity. There are very few activities where you have to bring these virtues into existence. To navigate through the problem presupposes we face ourselves through these virtues.

David: Can I add one more thing? Um, to me there is a readiness. At that moment for whatever reason—back at the original scene—she didn't have those qualities; she wasn't ready to deal with the situation. Something has changed between that point in time and the point in time last night when she said to herself, "I'm not taking the Tylenol. I'm ready for this thing."

Sophron: We're going to use what you just said in our exploration. This is the way we will do it. Notice our charts. These *are* present in a fictitious form. *These* are the real. There is a likeness of these, a likeness of these that now takes over, a likeness of these takes over. Let's see if we can make this clear.

Julie: In the past?

Sophron: Say, how did she appear when she gave that speech?

Julie: Totally in control, powerful, radiant, not radiant actually, but definite.

Sophron: Definite. Control. Ah, how does she appear in terms of those words we were just using?

Julie: All knowing.

Sophron: All knowing, wise, right? What else? She's not hesitant at all about giving this speech, or is she?

Julie: No, not at all hesitant.

Sophron: Telling you the reality as she knows it. Is she trying to be fair?

Julie: *She* thinks she is being fair.

Sophron: That is right. Notice, the problem exists because when she looked at her mother in this scene she was going to credit her mother with all of these virtues and they're all fictions.

David: Yeah, they're fictions, that is it!

Sophron: They are fictitious appearances of true virtues.

Julie: They are analogous to the real thing, but if we take *those* to be real...

David: That is the tension.

Sophron: That is the tension.

David: That is the tension that has to be resolved by yourself.

Sophron: That is right. OK, now, look!

Julie: So when I want to appear as a knower, I'm going to pick *her* as my model.

Sophron: That is right. Therefore, this image you have of yourself as knowing actually includes within it fictions and these are fictitious, mere copies that give the appearances of virtues.

Julie: I couldn't believe it; I was so surprised. I remember that sense of surprise that she didn't believe me. That was just– Still, it stings "It is like a what?! What do you mean it was nothing?!" Like I had that—for a split second—that desire to yell back at her, "What do you mean it was nothing?!" It blew me away. It was such a surprise to me that all of a sudden it turned out to be me instead of him being at fault and being yelled at by her. I got the sense that, "I'm not going to get any satisfaction at all, she doesn't even think it was his fault."

Sophron: Now let's go the next step, which is real curious. The image Julie gains of herself, would you agree, draws upon that past scene and possesses the very qualities that the mother appeared to have? Therefore, connected with this image are a set of qualities which the mother exhibited at that time, which you then accept to be real. Why? Why do we accept that as real?

David: Eases the tension.

Julie: If I don't then I have to take her on.

Sophron: Let's go over it.

Julie: I know where that goes. I already knew where that went, if I were to take her on and reject her view!

Sophron: Say, that was a pretty interesting scene you described with your mother, wasn't it? Would you agree we can probably construct a graph of how she appeared at different points of your life, can't we? By contrast, how did she appear when she wasn't in that kind of a state you just described? How did she appear to you then? Was that her everyday state? What was she like normally?

Julie: Absent.

Sophron: More. Concerned with you?

Julie: No.

Sophron: What?

Julie: Self absorbed. She had us convinced or she had me convinced that she just couldn't handle any more, that was always her, "I can't handle, I can't handle any more." I was the third of three kids, and my brother just taxed her to the limit. She used to say, "He just took everything I have, I don't have anything left. Leave me alone."

Sophron: With this description you can then establish what you might say is a kind of a baseline of normality, the way she usually is. That is what this line represents. And this high represents the way she revealed herself in that past scene at that time when she is telling you what she thinks. Is she not communicating with you at this time?

Julie: She is at least talking to me one-on-one.

Sophron: She broke through this flat line. She broke through this for a short period of time.

Julie: To convey to me something that she thought was pretty important.

Sophron: Therefore, in terms of her own experience with you? Finish it.

Julie: Well, I'll be! I just saw that in that moment she is sharing with me a major principle. Things are not as they seem! "Don't believe anything," she used to say. "Believe none of what you hear and half of what you see and you'll be all right."

Sophron: She's sharing principles of her reality.

Julie: What?

Sophron: That is right. She is sharing with you what she thinks is true about reality.

Julie: Right! What you think happened didn't happen, don't believe it.

Sophron: Right, that is what she is telling you. Therefore, this is called a dharma succession, passing on of the teachings. She is taking her whole experience and jamming it into a few words and handing it to you. It is a revealed teaching, her highest point in her life with you. It is memorable. She's never looked that good; she's never exhibited such qualities before. It is memorable.

Julie: I remember she was looking at me eye to eye.

Sophron: Eye to eye!

Julie: That was so rare that she would ever look at me like that; she was always distracted, so that is interesting. Yes indeed.

Sophron: Looks like the high point, the high point in your relationship. Now, if you call that phony, you have something to consider. Say, you know what?

Julie: What do you mean that I can't believe what I see or feel or experience?

Sophron: Then what are you rejecting? Her whole way of being, the whole dharma of her life, her whole teaching. It is a crisis. She is in a crisis because you may not agree, you have all the power. *Everyone who has a problem has all the power in the palm of their hand. The parent does not have it. The child has it. You have to deny what you see to have a problem and that means you have to close down your vision and take the belief to be true.* You knew what you experienced, therefore, when she is giving you this dharma transmission.

Julie: Let me tell you that now in the present when people do that to me, if they try to shut down my experience—my daughter will occasionally challenge my experience—I go ballistic. Oh man, there is nothing that makes me go more ballistic than to have somebody tell me that what I saw, that what I think I saw or whatever I heard, wasn't there!

Sophron: Brings this up, right? Does it bring this up?

Julie: Yeah, I think maybe the tones of voice.

Sophron: Now, are we elevating this scene as a high point in the family history? This is when you exist, Now you're seeing, *Now* you're someone, *now* you can be accepted. "*Now* I can share, *Now* I can tell you my truths, *Now* I will share with you what I personally have found out to be true about the nature of reality." This is monumental, and to suddenly turn around and say, "Bullshit, mom," you know? "I know what happened upstairs." It is gone, isn't it? You've got all the power. You have to have the power to have a problem.

Julie: I would have been hit if I had said that, though.

Sophron: Well, they may have done that.

Julie: I believed I would be hit because I saw her hit my sister, so I was pretty sure if I told her she was full of shit, I would get hit.

Sophron: I have talked with some people who came close to saying things like that and they got in very serious and curious accidents around the house.

Julie: Oooh that gives me Goosebumps. I remember a scene when I was four years old and my parents were about to go away on a trip and I saw something, and I wish I could remember what it was that I concluded.

Sophron: It was just out of reach?

Julie: I ran upstairs all excited to do something, and I fell and hit my eye on the corner of a dresser; and they had to rush me to the hospital, but see, they didn't do that to me.

Sophron: Yeah, but we'd like to know what you ran upstairs for. What was so important after hearing the family talk?

Julie: I had to get something off the top of the dresser that I wanted to give my parents before they went.

Sophron: Interesting. By the way how is your shoulder?

Julie: It doesn't hurt right now.

Helen: I think I missed part of the talk. Like at the last step of philosophical midwifery on the cover of the book, it says *meaning* and *naming*. Isn't that where you do a sound bite with your insight? Like you, you name your insight.

Sophron: *Yes. When you put the proper name on how the person is functioning you can begin the process of understanding. It is called the rectification of names.* You have to go from what you wanted to believe your mom was doing to realizing how she functioned. She appears virtuous and upstanding and supportive. She appears to be there for you and for this great moment. She's looking at you eye to eye, and she's sharing with you her most fundamental beliefs. Now you have to see how she was functioning. How is she really functioning?

Julie: She is a coward, actually. She's demonstrating cowardice because she is afraid to deal with my brother. So she pretends that the event is no big deal in order not to have to deal with it. So what is she doing? She's trying to pull the wool over my eyes, so she's deceptive

Sophron: Deceptive. What is another word? What was the word we were wondering about?

Julie: She's conning me.

Sophron: What? Conning? What was that word we were looking at on the tape, I forget what it was...

Julie: She's a fake.

Sophron: Your eyes are rather large now!

Julie: This is tough because it calls into question my self. Now, I'm not even sure I know when I'm being genuine, when I'm being fake.

Helen: There is a sense of freedom to it.

Sophron: There is no model! That is right! You lost your model!

Helen: But what I was looking for when I asked that question was to learn how that early scene connects with her present problem. I wasn't seeing the same words, but when she started to name what her mother really was, to rectify that, then I started to see some same language from the original problem statement.

Julie: Turn it back for a second.

Sophron: Now, let's go back and take a look at something.

Helen: Like cowardice?

Julie: I showed cowardice. I've done that to myself now that I think about it. It is like cotton, you know, like even wool.

Steve: You mentioned muffled I think.

Julie: Muffled, cotton, like I'm trying to pull the wool over my eyes. Like I don't want to see something.

Sophron: What did you call her at that moment?

Julie: Fake. Instead caring about me she was trying to protect her own view, save herself some work.

Sophron: Now we're naming.

Julie: But she didn't want to hear it.

Sophron: Now we go back to the original scene, we go back to our first sheet and we review it. Find anything curious about what it is we've been saying? Consider three states of mind.

Julie: I'm trying to find the right word to express it, that captures the whole belief that I walked away with. It was my fault. If I had just been able to find the right words, I would have been able to show her what really happened. So I walked away thinking it was my fault.

Sophron: We were right, then, in going for an expansion of that one term, weren't we?

Julie: So, I closed down rather than challenge it. I wonder what is in myself that I need to challenge, what is it that I'm closing down against, because there must be some corresponding seeing in my present life that I don't want to acknowledge or that I'm pushing away. I'm pushing it away, I'm disregarding it, I'm closing down rather than dealing with it. In the same way that I didn't deal with my mother, there is something that I'm doing to myself.

Sophron: True.

Steve: I think her model of dealing with it is what you're using to deal with it.

Sophron: Yes, that is right.

Julie: Her model of dealing with it. But I don't know what it is that I don't want to deal with in my present?

Sophron: That means we should be looking for something prior to the sleepless night of pain. Say, could you tell us, what was it like going into the motel last night? Got out of the car–

Julie: I was very sleepy, very tired, I went right in and went to sleep. I made it sound like I never got to sleep, but I went right to sleep and I woke up two hours later, and then I didn't sleep very much for the rest of the night. But that was– I did– I was so exhausted I went right to sleep.

Sophron: Then you woke up in this state.

Julie: I woke up in this state and I had a dream and I couldn't get it; it was just out of my reach! It was the same exact thing, I could not get it!

Sophron: Wouldn't it be nice if you had that dream now.

Julie: I've been recording my dreams for five years. It is not like I don't have any experience at being able to get them, but this one was gone before I could even put one word on it!

Steve: Remember what we were talking about when I dropped you off at the hotel?

Julie: No.

Sophron: You don't remember what you were talking about? Think about it for a moment.

Julie: As a matter of fact, this was bothering me this morning, too, because I was trying to reflect on the entire dialogue that we had last night and most of it was gone. And it was very disturbing to me that in trying to practice a certain amount of Pythagorean recollection in the morning, trying to remember what I did the day before and what was said, and it is just out of my reach! I feel like if somebody just gave me a little hint it would all just come brrrr. It would all just come flying out, but that right now there is something blocking it.

Sophron: The reason I interrupted you is to see whether we could get part of this drama back. Continue, please.

Steve: Well I asked that question because I remember what we were talking about, and it may have triggered something, and I didn't want to say it because if she is not the one bringing it back, then–

Sophron: In a Pythagorean philosophical community their practice was that in the mornings, before they did anything, they would walk around together and they would ask one another any question they wanted about the preceding day, and it was completely free and open. So, we'll invoke this Pythagorean principle and say we are a community, and you have the right to express it if you'll accept that role.

Julie: Oh yes, definitely.

Steve: I'll just ask the question, then. What do you think life is all about?

Julie: Ha ha!!

Sophron: Oh! Ah! And what is life all about? By god, go ahead!

Steve: She asked me first, and I told her what I thought it was. And then I asked her, and she was talking about that when I dropped her off at the hotel.

Sophron: Go ahead.

Julie: Oh, yes, I was telling him that I thought that the only place we can learn, the only place we're nurtured is here on earth, and it fascinated me that the soul takes with it into the next world only what it learns, education and nurture. But it is a particular kind of learning and nurturing, and I was telling him that some of it can be found in Plato's Republic in the studies for the philosopher king; you have to go through certain reflective activity, a certain type of activity that trains the mind to reach for and to see in its own mind, in mind, ultimate reality. You want to train yourself to focus on what is real.

Helen: You're using the same words as the pathologos. I hear you using—

Steve: Focus on, reach for.

Helen: Reach for, what you learn; what you learned from your mother, you take that with you.

Julie: But I was unsatisfied with this when I left the car.

Helen: Ultimate reality, just out of reach.

Julie: When I left the car I was unsatisfied with our discussion. I remember feeling that it was unfinished, that there was something wrong with it, that we hadn't, and yet, as soon as I walked into the hotel, it was gone!

Helen: You forgot.

Julie: It was wiped out, and I don't remember your answer, which distresses me even more as to what you think life is all about.

David: The truth is the tension never dissipates.

Sophron: That is right; until you surface it, question it, that is right. You were going to–

Julie: I wanted to remember what his answer was to what life was all about.

Sophron: And?

Julie: I don't remember at all!

Sophron: Well, he's right here, I happen to know him. Steve, Julie.

Steve: Let's see if I can remember what I said.

Julie: Or just give us a fresh answer.

Steve: Basically life is all about God experiencing ourselves, experiencing itself more fully as us, through us, meeting itself, in all myriads of ways that are possible, given form and interaction.

Julie: We had talked earlier about multiplicity and manifestation and how something comes to be at the same time that it is thought of, and you said on the way from the airport, "That– That is God getting to know itself in every one of its multiple aspects. It wants to see itself, so it is played out." And, so my concern, I remember part of the concern for me in this whole thing is– What is life about for *me*? I want to see some particular, I want to see– Oh my goodness! This is bringing some emotion.

Sophron: Go on, "I want to see some particular..."

Julie: I want to see myself, I want to see something particular, that I have some particular flowering that is me.

Sophron: Yes

Julie: And, what is that?

Sophron: And, therefore, when Steve suggested it was god experiencing himself, what did that mean to you?

Julie: I don't know.

Sophron: Did it confirm it? Did it support it? Was it parallel to it? Similar?

Julie: No, it changes the question. If every manifestation is God getting to know himself, seeing himself, then I'm also something that God is taking a look at, right?

Sophron: And?

Julie: What does he see? What is that? What is being seen?

Sophron: What does it do to your interest, though?

Julie: What does it do to my interest?

Sophron: Remember you said you were interested in particularity, what you're experiencing.

Julie: Sometimes I know I'm in touch with reality when I act in a certain– There is a certain state of mind where activity becomes fluid and effortless and there is a beauty to it, and it is when I reflect on that kind of activity that I see that those are the moments that I am most being myself, being myself at my fullest.

Sophron: Yes.

Julie: When I'm not restricted. So I guess life is all about cultivating that way of being where I can act out in that natural way, that we were talking about just before, with virtue.

Sophron: *As you reflect on the story with her mother, what was her mother revealing at that time? A whole philosophy of life, was she not sharing something? Something similar going on when she got in the car and came out of the car. Is there something similar going on between the two? Reflect.*

Julie: Right, in some way I want to wipe out what he said.

Sophron: Because?

Julie: Because if God is seeing his own mind in everything that exists and I'm one of those things, then something particular about me is good.

Sophron: But do you remember what attitude you had or the state of mind when you heard Steve's remark

Julie: I forgot it. I guess I wiped it out.

Sophron: I was just wondering. *What she concluded from that scene, could it possibly be similar to that earlier scene?*

Julie: I did leave the car thinking that I hadn't expressed what I was seeing very well and that I wanted to be able to share it more fully.

Sophron: Perhaps all you needed, then, were the proper words. Maybe if you had the right words to it, then you'd be able to understand it?

Julie: I went further than that. My understanding of it was weak.

Sophron: *See what we are we doing?*

David: Recreating the tension.

Sophron: *Structural similarity of the pathologos, it is called. Since the inception of the pathologos has a certain dramatic structure, wherever one finds oneself in a similar situation, to that degree you are likely to play out the same role, in the same manner, to the same conclusion and suffer the same loss. Hence there is a likeness or symmetry to the original transmission.*

David: Since we're all exposed at some point to a great deception by people we love and trust.... we're all going to have a problem.

Sophron: *There is no one who is not going to have a problem for two simple reasons.*

Julie: We're intelligent, that is one.

Sophron: *And unless you have a parent who is so exceedingly wise that they can tell you the truth about the nature of reality [much laughter] heh, and with such clarity and precision of words that there is not the slightest hint of ambiguity, you'll have a problem. And the child must be in the most receptive state of mind to hear those words and allow them to enter into himself. If as a child you can find a proper response deep within your own soul so that you can naturally absorb them and become akin with that person who is sharing it with you, and therefore you have the same virtues as the spokesman, the transmitter, then you can put all those things together; but you still need one more thing. You'd better not walk away with the thought that they're better than you. You– Whatever image is created of yourself at that moment better be consistent; otherwise, you see, there is no image of the self that you can have that is any good. Because you take a look at the nature of the self, there is no image that can in any way even approximate its nature.*

Julie: And yet that is what we're looking for in this question.

Sophron: True.

Steve: One last comparison, just to compare the two events. What if what happened in that old event really did happen, and you had a perfect understanding of what actually occurred. It was the subsequent handling of that situation which caused you to question it. Perhaps there is a similarity about who you are right now. Maybe you understand perfectly well and articulating it is not the problem.

Sophron: That is right. What if you really did disagree with what someone was saying and it had nothing to do with a failure on your part to find proper words.

Julie: Yeah, oh my goodness, I was disagreeing with him? Oh my goodness!

Sophron: [Laughs]

Julie: Oh my goodness! I never saw it that way. Oh my goodness, that is what happened, though, that is what– Oh my goodness!

Sophron: So?

Julie: When I'm thinking I'm disagreeing with someone, I don't want to do that, I don't. It is unacceptable. That has to be–

Sophron: In that scene could you disagree with your mother?

Julie: It is being replaced by something else. It has to be replaced by something else. It has to be replaced by something else when I'm going to disagree with someone. I was noticing, see, that was one of the things that I was going to tell you about the way we interacted for this whole day, and I started to tell you a little bit about it in there. I wasn't able to put the right words on it yet, but I was admiring the conviction of your ability to state where you're at and what you're experiencing and what you're willing to take and what you're not willing to take, what you're willing to agree with and what you don't agree with, what you see and what you don't see. And you're so clear about it, and so I was admiring that, but I think it is because–

Helen: No, no not the–

Sophron: Parallel to what?

Julie: Such a conflict, though, with what I do when I see that I don't agree with someone. I either have to disregard what they say—

Sophron: Push away?

Julie: Or get mad or something. I'm not able to just cleanly say I disagree.

Sophron: You're doing it now.

Julie: I think it is this way. Oh, I don't know.

Sophron: Let me see whether I can pull some images together for a few minutes and have a little fun. Would you agree, there was something on your mother's mind?

Julie: How to protect my daughter from seeing.

Sophron: And what was interesting about it is that it had a certain brilliance to it, right? And now there you are, and you're dealing with your own mind and that past event. Her teachings bounce off the wall of the cave of your own mind.

David: Oh, I see.

Sophron: Recall the words that your mother said in that past scene. It is as if these words are bouncing off the wall of your mind. You don't recall them as hers, and you accept them as your own creations. These are the voices that you say to yourself, but we need to remind you that they're merely echoes of what she has said to you many years ago. These echoes we assume express our innermost self because they come from within us. They seem so vivid and real, but you forget that what gives them their brilliance is the carefully crafted appearance of truth, sincerity, and clarity that she gave them. She made those words seem so true because if she didn't convince you, she would have to deal with something she couldn't even challenge. She is the one that is carrying something aloft for you to see—and in seeing and hearing to accept as reality. The words alone couldn't do it. The need to shine them before you brings you to a new awareness of her, for she is showing herself as she seldom does. Indeed, it is as if her words were glowing with truth and sincerity. Consider. Isn't this what makes it seem as if it is shining in truth? These images on the wall of your mind are made visible by the light that shines behind those words. We can imagine that this luminosity to be like a fire that shines behind you but which you never turn around to see because you have fixed your attention on those flittering images on the wall of your mind. It is the same for everyone, as long as a person accepts those voices to be an expression of their own nature they will be guided by them and enchained and unable to free themselves of their folly. And these images? Do you know what they are? They are the stuff out of which she and others like her use to craft an image acceptable to her. It is a mask that has a role and drama to play out and for this performance she will extend a kind of love. She is crafting an image for you to believe, and the moment you accept it you put it on and lose your original face.

Few people can challenge all this by themselves because they have taken it to be real. However, if someone were to ask these prisoners of the mind a few questions, they just might be able to break free of their chains. You might frame a few questions such as, "Say, those voices and images you say are central to yourself? Is it at all possible that you've heard things like that before? Those voices now, is it possible that they have a certain tone to them? An attitude that just might go along with them? Could you reflect on when you might have heard someone you know acting this way, saying these kinds of things? Now, these echoes and images you experience can you describe when they seem to have an urgency to them? What might you have been doing when you heard these inner voices and felt the presence of these images or shadows? Is it possible that these shadows and echoes came from people you might have thought of in your youth as having an honored position, someone higher and more noble appearing than yourself? And is it possible that these things that you experience in your mind are the "man made things" that they seem to carry on the top of their heads?

Consider. Are not these trusted authorities trying in every way to make as vivid and clear to you their message? Do they not want you to accept as your reality what is present before you under pain that if it is refused, love itself and respect will be withheld? What do we have here but Plato's allegory of the cave and the upper world? You recall that he says that we have been enchained since our youth in such a way that we can't turn around to see the source of these images or the echoes that bounce off the walls of the cave; neither can we discover the fire that casts reflections on the wall of the cave. Further, he says, we are so chained that we cannot see one another because our necks have been chained in such a way as to force us to see only the shadows reflected on the wall of the cave.

Julie: That is just what it feels like.

Sophron: That is the way Plato describes the allegory of the cave and the upper world.

Julie: That's what I'm striving to do, to be able to hold on to what I see, to be able to express it clearly, not to back down into the cave, to not do that, to not slouch over and hump over and pretend that I'm weak and stupid.

Sophron: Yes. When you recall this discussion and reflect upon it you will see even more than you have because turning the mind upon its own puzzles brings to birth an understanding we need for our own development.

Julie: I guess it stands to reason that that would come up. Thank you very much.

Sophron: Thank you for volunteering and being willing to explore a problem you didn't think you had. We said: maybe we'll take something that isn't a random thought and see whether we can find something in it that is a problem.

David: Indeed.

Sophron: HA! You see what sedating will do? It'll rob you of your problem. Well, thank you all for participating in our dialogue. Let me go around and thank each of our speakers for participating.

Joseph: *Sophron went around shaking hands with everyone. And he seemed to have something to say to each.*

The Symmetry, Part 4: Sophron and Harry

> Joseph: *As the others left, Harry hung back obviously anxious to talk to Sophron about something.*

Harry: Well, Sophron, I can't say I didn't find your talk interesting.

Sophron: What can you say?

Harry: Frankly, I don't know what to say because I'm not sure what went on here. Was it a lucky fluke, a random set of factors coming together, so it sounded like there is something rational going on? It is not that I can't say I was wrong, since I'm not at all sure of what went down here. It's like watching something you don't believe can happen, and it happens in front of you. I find it, somehow, disturbing, that's what. And whatever success you think you might have is because you were lucky enough to have had Steve present. He brought up facts, real facts I might say, that she forgot and that's what finally tied it all together. And I'm not sure what that means either.

Sophron: You are right again, Harry. Steve's account shows most clearly why this kind of work, what we call philosophical midwifery, works best within a community of seekers. It is the old Pythagorean brotherhood idea returning once again. If societies foster and promote spiritual development through rational, scientific procedures, they will naturally be drawn to philosophical midwifery. You see, Harry, if problems are produced from, and in, irrational societies, like the episodes within the family, they can be disassembled in and through rational societies. If it could only happen in churches, brotherhoods, guilds, or this or that kind of society, you can be sure it will transform both the individual and the nature of the group itself. The forces that created the urgency to accept false beliefs can also bring about the very conditions needed to challenge their existence and power.

Harry: Are you so bold to claim that all forms of therapy, counseling, and religious movements need this technique of yours? Is your ego that inflated?

Sophron: Perhaps it is as you say, but try another direction. Why not consider the obvious? Man is not rational, but he can become rational, and that is only if he learns how to be rational. It is possible to bring rationality into man's various activities, but only if we have discovered how to introduce it into those activities. The forces against the introduction of reason are formidable, but it is, at least in principle, possible to do so if we can discover and can use rational models.

The culture we have inherited from Europe has been convinced that man is irrational, driven by instinctual urges, and whatever rationality man does possess is regarded as only a veneer, a mask that covers his irrational nature. Reason is believed to be much like a computer, something that processes logical structures but is impotent and incapable of nurturing man.

Take a look at the various forms of psychotherapy. They all assume that purely rational procedures are ineffective in helping man reach a state of being that is both rational and free of conflict. Our culture is willing to try anything if it offers even a slim chance of being able to change man for the better and that includes drugs, starvation, electric shock treatments, prefrontal lobotomy, and inculcating beliefs, but the only thing it can't imagine might be beneficial is the cultivation of reason; simply because they don't know what it is.

We can also see this play itself out in those religions that believe man is fundamentally flawed, a sinner, and in need of redemption through belief; for if rational procedures were sufficient, then Christ died in vain—to paraphrase Paul.

Indeed, philosophy is no stranger to this tradition since the various schools of European philosophy can be classified and defined in terms of the degree to which they turn their backs upon the purely rational. The academic world is no different. They mirror European thought, are afraid to present the purely rational as a spiritual unified vision because they themselves lack any expertise in what they have ignored. Strangers to the mind they become scholars of those who repudiate the mind. But Harry, reason hasn't failed philosophy, religion, and psychology, since they haven't even sought for rational models. Hence, this is merely a prejudice against the mind, and the denial of the reach of its various cognitive functions.

Harry: Why do you say that? Oh, I see what you are saying. I heard you say it before. I don't believe I ever grasped it before, but I do now. Your idea of the purely rational is a Platonic yoga, a kind of pure intellectual *jñāna* yoga at that, and that makes you a religious mystic.

Sophron: The way you put it sounds like a criticism. But Harry, the idea of connecting mysticism with religion misses the mark because one gains membership in a religion by accepting their beliefs, and not by the cultivation of some spiritual practice. However, mystics go their own ways, they craft their own beliefs from their own experiences, and they take the direction of their lives from what is revealed to them rather than from a body of beliefs. Harry, have you forgotten that Socrates calls himself a mystic in the *Phaedo* and says that he has left nothing undone to become one of them?

Harry: I imagine you have a quote for everything, but that doesn't prove much. Wait a minute! Just what do you understand to be the end of this "purely rational" approach, this Platonic thing you've cooked up?

Sophron: Man is rational. The fullest flowering of the mind can be nurtured and developed through a Platonic vision of Philosophy. Indeed, even a single ray of its brilliance is enough to awaken thinkers. It may not be known as it should, but Augustine and Thomas Aquinas were both indebted to Platonic thinkers, and without them they could not have developed their systems. Without those deep and nourishing roots they are left with empty rituals and a religious rhetoric that has lost its meaning.

Actually, if we are to speak accurately we should say that there is no Platonic philosophy or tradition because it is really a rational vision that leads to the unfoldment of mind that culminates in a vision of the nature of reality. If anyone accepts that it is possible to participate in this realm, and from such experience can infer the ideas and categories necessary to build a coherent system, then they are pursuing a rational, reflective philosophy that some can call Platonic. Others would say they are merely using their own mind.

Harry: So that's it, isn't it? For you Plato is the paradigm. You would rewrite history, wouldn't you?

Sophron: No, but someone might enjoy writing man's struggle to become rational. Such a historian would, I hope, begin with Homer and place him at the threshold of understanding, because it was he who saw so clearly that in the struggle to achieve one's destiny, it was essential to emerge from the pathologos of the family and society.

Harry: I can't believe it. You are really trying to credit these ancient Greeks with that kind of sophisticated vision? Should I laugh or simply ignore what you are saying? Haven't you heard that Homer is prehistory? Are you going to save Homer by trying to convince me that these myths are archetypal images of man's spiritual development? Do you have your own secret way of reading meaning into Greek myths like Jung and Joseph Campbell? Because if that's coming just count me out. Well, if that's what's going to happen, don't call me, I'll call you. Look, if you are into the mind, as you seem to be, just what are you into myth for?

Sophron: If you make the time to delve into these issues, I would welcome exploring them with you. As it is now it seems to me that we are only trading views on a variety of subjects and not treating any of them with the attention and care they deserve. Consider the subject you just brought up, the issue of the nature of the mind and mythology: Shall we be like returning tourists in a competition to see whose photos of some foreign land are best?

Harry: You know, Sophron, you place too high a significance on reason, that's all. Consciousness is where it is at, experiencing the heightened state of the moment, to hold fast to it and drink it up. Reason is a thinking tool and that's good, but one day we might have a computer chip grafted to the brain to improve its performance.

Sophron: But if reason is like a computer chip, what is it that has the intelligence to use these computer chips?

Harry: What do you really believe to be this thing you call mind and to what higher use do you believe it can be put other than calculating and planning?

Sophron: Perhaps, there are times when trading answers without being clear about the reasons for them is necessary; however, I'll put a condition on mine. Let's talk about this issue again but only after you have read Socrates' Speech in the *Symposium* because there you will find the role of the mind discussed in a very clear and simple way. Because there he states that it is only through the mind that a vision of reality can be had. If you hold on to that idea for awhile, you will see that he is making a claim that mind is not merely a thinking tool but it is only through this eye of the soul, mind, that reality can be experienced.

Harry: Experienced, you say?

Sophron: Yes, experienced. It really does come down to whether or not one can verify in one's own experience that it is through the mind only that one secures a vision of Beauty in itself. For it is in the experience of beauty itself that one recognizes that truth or reality is that Intelligible Beauty. Again, for those fortunate enough to gain that vision some go further to discover that its source is none other than the One or the Good.

Harry: Am I hearing that you believe Plato can rival our spiritual systems? That it can compete with our Judaic-Christian traditions? You know, I bet you can't find anything parallel to that in Plato's own writings. Plato could never have thought that his dialogues would compete with Homer and Hesiod, right?

Sophron: It is there, don't bet. It is in that magnificent speech of Socrates in the *Symposium*. What is said to be born between Diotima and Socrates, the philosopher, "would look to Homer and Hesiod, and the other good poets, and wish to rival them." Very prophetic remark of Plato's; I often recall that passage with fondness.

Harry: I'd like to know what you believe will happen if there is such a turn to Platonic thought.

Sophron: Harry, since the signs of every Platonic revival was called a renaissance, we can say it is happening in front of you. Now, I am not saying you should prepare for a flood, but you might enjoy getting your feet wet in one of its streams.

The Symmetry, Part 5: Raymond and Joseph

Raymond: I agree with Harry. I don't know what to think about the conference, and that goes double for that last dialogue. And as for you, that was some recollection. I knew that as an actor you somehow learned to memorize a play at record speed, but I hadn't anticipated this. How did it all end? Did some discussion go on after the conference was over?

Joseph: You are right. The dialogue was audio recorded, and I listened to it so often that I convinced myself that I should go the next step and memorize it. Now I go around and recite the whole as if it were a single workshop talk. I'll tell you that it is more fun than I ever found in acting. As for the discussion that followed, well, there sure were talks. I can't tell you all of them, of course, but Dion and Sophron got together, and from what I heard it must have been a really thought provoking talk about Proclus and Pseudo-Dionysius. Steve and Mike talked into the night. Then Ionia and Helen got into a talk about the spiritual life and love, and Harry and Julie went off to discuss something in private. Sometime later I heard that Sophron and Steve explored the implications of the possible use of psychedelic drugs in the Eleusinian mysteries, but I haven't learned what conclusions they reached. I had a talk with Sophron about the Hellenic idea of prayer and later used it in my talk with Harry.

Raymond: Frankly, Joseph, I'll bet the talk between Ionia and Helen was a flight into fantasy land. I wager the talks Sophron had were worth whatever you had to pay to hear them.

Joseph: Because?

Raymond: Because saints don't get laid, that's what. Raise up the mind and put down the virility. Everyone who pursues Heaven is at war with their own sexuality. And your dear friend Plato was no different.

Joseph: Since you seem to have all the issues added up together, do you think that this strangest of all philosophers, Socrates, avoided sexuality, too? His wife had his child, and he was at least 70 years old at the time.

Raymond: You know that's the razor's edge for me. Quoting Plato doesn't change a thing. Actually, I'm baffled why anyone would believe that returning to Platonic dialogues could make anyone more rational. The roots of man's irrationality are too deep and mysterious. It is just impossible to believe you can find a remedy for it in some writings of Plato. It just doesn't make any sense, that's all. You might just as well believe that in resurrecting the Gods of Greece you can reform Christendom.

Joseph: Yet here you are, and even you do go in and out of showing an interest in this stuff, don't you?

Raymond: It was only after I heard that you got involved in all this that I became curious about it.

Joseph: And what turned that curiosity into coming down here?

Raymond: Well, I did hear Michelle say that she learned how to understand her own dreams by following this way of analysis, so when I laughed at this she gave me an audio tape of one of her dream-analysis talks and challenged me to study them myself.

Joseph: So that's how you got here. And now?

Raymond: Well, after this dialogue between Sophron and Julie, I'd say everything just jumped a couple of levels. I'll even deal with the possibility that this approach might work with some dreams, some waking problems, and even some pains and some random happenings in our life. I just don't know what that means. It is like someone asking you to search through a garbage dump and pull out what you threw away many years ago. There is something about it that is not fair. I'll go for any other solution, not this.

Joseph: And what about the idea of the Dream Master, Raymond?

Raymond: I figured who cares if someone gets poetic and makes up another catchy name. Just shrug 'em off and go your own way. Maybe I don't like the idea of talking about an idea as if it were a person; that's too anthropomorphic for me. Just because there is a way to see dreams as rational doesn't mean that there is a person sitting around making up a multimedia show for you, you know? It doesn't take much to persuade kids that there is only one Santa Claus, even though they see those men dressed as Santa Claus all around, but try it on older kids and you'll find it won't work. So each of us may have our own multimedia master, and that means there are many masters, not one.

Joseph: Very good point there, Raymond, and as a matter of fact I recently heard Harry and Sophron discussed this very issue. I'm interested in finding out how it went; and after I find out, I'll pass it on to you if you are interested in it.

Raymond: Actually, I'm only somewhat interested in that one-many problem. You know what has happened to all those logical proofs of the existence of God, don't you? Is it at all possible to offer something other than phony proofs that really prove the existence of something you can only guess about?

Joseph: I'm still guessing, but I think that having the right questions helps to focus your mind on the right issue, doesn't it?

Raymond: Sure it does, Joseph. You know Allan Hartley. Well, he and I had a talk, and he urged me to look into some of these issues and into these conferences. You know that he ran a few articles on this dialoguing stuff a few years ago in his New Perspectives journal, and he wants to keep in touch with where it is going. But I'm in a quandary about what to write. Look at it this way: I'd say that Sophron seems to know just what question will keep the person searching along with him for an answer. What guides that questioning process is what I'd like to know.

Joseph: And it does seem to work with dreams, problems, and even things like pains and random doings, doesn't it? There is something about it that is curious, isn't there? How do you see it?

Raymond: I don't believe that kind of thing can be taught anywhere, and I sure don't think you can get it by just going out and practicing the process. I will probably say it's a gift. Like, it comes to some and not to others, and no one can figure out why it comes when it does.

Joseph: Maybe not, but one thing is true about it: people benefit from it. As for teaching this stuff, I just don't know much about that, but I've heard from other talks that major changes would have to take place before this could be taught and practiced as an art in our colleges and universities. For myself, I think when we made the deal to separate the church from the state we, unknowingly, separated education from meaning. Just try this on for size: Do you think school boards would recommend that their schools introduce periods of meditation if research showed that a period of meditation before learning improves learning? No way; they would look over their shoulder at their local churches in fear of making such a decision. Let's change things around and make sure teachers are on the boards of the churches since they influence school boards. What the heck can you say? Schools are emasculated centers for informing students of facts not centers of art, music and transformative programs.

I imagine it is all part of our society accepting the thesis that the mind, emotions, and spirit of man are three separate realms; and while there may be a unity to them, each is really separate and distinct from the others. Now this art of philosophical midwifery reaches through them all—so that no one knows how to deal with it or where it should be practiced and learned. As for how one person can do it and another not? That is a good question, too.

Raymond: Frankly, from what I've heard I'd say that whatever else you need that having a bit of luck on your side to pull it off won't hurt. It was luck that her pain had a mental component to it, because as you know it didn't have to, did it?

Joseph: I don't think so, but I sure would like to know if it could be otherwise.

Raymond: It is very difficult for me to even imagine so many people being wrong, and you guys right. That's all. You are offering what can't be true, you know that? Well, at least you agree that a bit of luck helps along the process. Say, since you've had talks with Sophron, what does he call it?

Joseph: He calls it a kind of wisdom, because whenever wisdom is added to anything it makes it helpful and leads to some kind of good.

Raymond: So wisdom finally comes home to roost. It is a word I seldom have a need for but it may fit here.

Joseph: Then can we say that what we have seen is a rational method guided by a kind of wisdom, which leads to a good for those to whom it comes?

Raymond: Yes.

Joseph: Would you go further and say that when reason leads this way, it reveals the roots of one's ignorance, doesn't it?

Raymond: So that's what Sophron is trying to show, the presence of a revealing wisdom. That's it, then, right?

Joseph: Yes. If it fits the individual most perfectly it would mean there is a symmetry between the wisdom of the Dream Master and its application to each one of us.

Raymond: Now, I find that astonishing, don't you? Frankly I go in and out of this discussion; sometimes I'm following and sometimes I'm not, and now I don't know which I'm doing.

Joseph: But you are no stranger to reflecting and speculating, Raymond, so what is it that pulls you out of these reflections? Because you are into it, and then you pull out, right?

Raymond: It comes down to the fact that each of us has to put aside these reflections and face the fact that each of us sees things from our own private viewpoint, that's what. We only know what's going on in our own minds. We're glued to the TV of our own mind, and we can't turn around to see anything but the channel we're facing. And no one can turn around and see themselves viewing the screen. We are really locked in and chained to the images we project on the screen of our own mind. So I take a ride through these reflections and come down to earth when I remind myself that it's not real and that sure pulls me down and fast.

Joseph: Say, Raymond, Sophron used to say that some thoughts are like echoes that we keep listening to and that they have a kind of power that makes us pay attention to them. If that's so, can you recall some earlier scene when you were urged to be this or that?

Raymond: No way. I'm not into that kind of talk. Why don't you just tell me how it ended: Did Sophron have anything else to say before ending it all?

Joseph: Yes, he did. He added something else. He said now that we can appreciate what the Dream Master does, we should try to discover what it is in itself. If we don't discover that, he said, we will be ignorant of the source and nature of what guides us. He added something curious, and I've been thinking about it since he asked me the question, "If what guides the Dream Master is also a kind of wisdom, then how does it differ from the wisdom that guides Sophron's talks and the kind we just went through?" Now, I have been puzzling over this kind of question, and I wonder if you might want to explore this idea with me.

Raymond: I think I have had my fill, Joseph. Thanks for the recollection. I've got enough to think about. I'm not sure what I'm going to do with it all, but I do know I'm going to have a couple of cups of coffee with Alan Hartley about all this.

Birthing a Prayer: A Dialogue Play

Harry: I will make it simple for you. It is not a mystery; it is obvious to everyone but you. You ought to know by now that the way of devotion is from the heart and not from intellect. What the heart needs the mind denies. It's not possible to reconcile this conflict. As someone once said, "The heart has its reasons which the mind cannot comprehend." And that's all there is to it.

Joseph: I don't believe it, that's all. Why can't the demands of the heart be in harmony with the mind? Do you really believe that there is a split or rupture in the fabric of Man so that we have to keep them separate? I don't believe they have to feud and destroy one another.

Harry: They are different and they function differently, too. Reason by definition lacks feeling; it is cold and indifferent to what is essential in being human. Reason is just a computer, no feeling, and no love. You've heard the story of Adam and Eve and you know what brought about the fall, don't you?

Joseph: Belief in myths must be part of your faith not mine. Read the story again and you'll see only Adam, not Eve, was sent out of the Garden. I'll tell you, you don't even care to know what directs your devotion. What if the demands of reason undermine devotion? Then all that went into devotion may be mistaken and empty.

Harry: Joseph, not everything in a myth is mythical; they can contain some truth. Mistaken and empty to you, that is. Look at it my way and ask if the reverse is equally true. If the demands of devotion expose the limitations of reason then is not reason blind and empty? Well, maybe for something you might bring the mind and heart together, but from what I have seen it is not possible in devotion. It's simple. When its time for devotion you want unity, and that means you must silence what brings division and strife. We are not going to agree on this, and I just recalled I have an appointment I have to keep. Maybe we can continue this sometime later.

Joseph: Wait a minute! There is Sophron. Let's call him over; he might be able to help. We have been going around and around on this point long enough.

BIRTHING A PRAYER 77

Harry: No, not me. I've heard him before, and he just complicates just about everything with his questions and metaphors. That's all he does. So long.

Joseph: Hey there Sophron, care to join me. As you see Harry left in a bit of a hurry. I was trying to discuss an issue with him that I know you have discussed many times before, but I don't know if you have heard this version of it. At least I think it is another form of the One-Many problem.

Sophron: You are a scoundrel, Joseph. Here I was on my way to something I thought important and you bait your trap with a One-Many problem. Well, I am here, and as you know I am always intrigued to learn a new version of the One-Many problem. But let me warn you that I have never been able to persuade myself that I have reached a genuine solution to even one of these problems.

Joseph: What are you talking about? You must have concluded something through all your talk about these problems. I have been present in some of these talks and I heard you come to many a conclusion, and good ones, too, or so I thought at the time. You have been at it for a long time. But me? I'm somewhat new at it, but I just love the fun you can have with it.

Sophron: True, it does offer a playful way of reasoning. Sure you can get some fun that way. The higher end of it is still playful, and it is sometimes called the Noblest Game. As for me I think you have overestimated my skill in this game. You have only seen the half of it. After those talks are over I reflect on them, and I see that I concluded too hastily. Much to my surprise I found again and again that when I thought I knew something, I wasn't even close to knowing. So the conclusions I have reached at those times seem to vanish away like the early morning mist. It is because I just can't seem to convince myself that the answers I have reached are true. So you might want to talk with someone else about this if you want to reach the truth about these things; only please tell me the new form of this One-Many problem you encountered with Harry.

Joseph: Not unless you agree to explore it with me. I want to convince Harry and his group that when the heart and the mind are at odds with one another, it is the mind that has the veto power over the heart. Look Sophron, let me lay it out for you. You see, Harry's group says that

God is one and is all there is; and I told him that if that is true, then the God that is-all-there-is must be a many and not a one. So a God that is many can't be a one that's for sure. So what? Well, that kind of monism is in reality a polytheism. Those who believe such things aren't really interested in understanding what they are saying; they just want to feel good saying whatever they say, and they sure don't want someone around telling them that they don't make any sense. For how could what is one be many?

Sophron: Indeed, you found me out. I'm hooked, you caught me. You are indeed a brave man to challenge and demand clarity on such a lofty issue. It must be because your teacher has inspired you with his way of teaching. What was his name? Oh yes, it was Fill—f-i-l-l—Eristics.

Joseph: There you go with your names. You know the name of my teacher and it is not Fill it is Phil—p-h-i-l—and his last name is Smothers as you know.

Sophron: You are right, I forgot his name and somehow got it mixed up with another one. Isn't he the one who argues that there can be no communication between man and God because God needs nothing man has and man wants everything God has? I think he concluded that all prayer, sacrifice and petitions to God were hollow and empty pleadings.

Joseph: That's right. The way he argued it out was that in an uncaring universe there is no God worthy of your prayers. I was trying to persuade Harry of the futility of prayers. Let me tell you how the argument went and the points that I made. I thought they were really good at the time and I think so now. I'd like to get your reaction to what I took Harry through.

Sophron: Before you go into all that, I have one little thing I would like to clear up before we begin. Tell me, Joseph, when you use the term one which of the ones are you talking about?

Joseph: Why are you raising that kind of question?

Sophron: Well if someone were to say that God is one we might ask which of the many ideas of one is God one? Since there are many ideas of one, we would want to know which one of the many is being referred to. And if there are several ideas of one I would imagine someone would want to assign the best one to God if they say God is one.

Joseph: Sure, there may be different ideas of one, but they are all the same if each is one. So what makes you think that if you say God is one that the one you are referring to might be better than another idea of one?

Sophron: Suppose you find that among the different ideas of one there is one that is more profound than all the others; and if that is true, then I would imagine that when you say that God is one, that you would have the more profound idea in mind rather than the others. That's all.

Joseph: Sophron, just what are you talking about? How can one idea of one be more profound than another idea of one? But whatever you call one must be the same, so how can you possibly say that one of the many is better or more profound than another?

Sophron: Let's review a few things first. Can we agree that all the things on this table are a collection of things? And when we say a collection, we mean one collection of all those things? Again, Joseph, when we say each is one of the things in the collection we are saying each is one, are we not? Look at the box of matches. It is one of the things on the table. Isn't it a one that has many matches within it? Further, each of the matches has no special place in the box, and each is a one and in one box.

Joseph: Sure, that's obvious.

Sophron: See, there is a book; it is one of many parts woven together into a unity? Yet, the parts: Each page is not like those parts in our collection, is it? Because each has a place and fits into an order, and that order and arrangement is what makes the pages into a book rather than merely a collection of pages. Do you agree? And when that special collection of pages comes together, a new thing emerges and we call it a book?

Joseph: Wait a minute. In all the talks I've heard about the One-Many I never heard this idea of a new thing coming into existence out of a one. Curious. Where are you going with it?

Sophron: Let's take another example first. Take a look at the watch you are wearing. Isn't it true that all the parts are in some special interrelationship, or unity? Sure, each of the parts is no less a one, but each also functions or interrelates with other parts in its own specially designed way. Now, is it not true that the parts of the watch function differently from those that make up the book? And when all the parts of the watch function properly, they not only produce a working watch, but its unity can be used to measure time?

Joseph: And the unity produces a new thing out of its many parts, right?

Sophron: Yes. Again, as you consider it would you say that there is a different kind of unity of the parts of a healthy body from that of the watch? Since in the body each of the organs of the body must each function in a different yet ideal way as well as functioning together ideally, or otherwise there would be illness instead of health. Is that not so?

Joseph: I see what you are getting at, but the kinds of ones you describe are different and they are still ones. I'm not sure where this is going. You know that there are times that you just might tell me what you think instead of going through all these steps. Why not just give me the answer I need, and then I can go on to tell you about my talk with Harry.

Sophron: I think you are asking why I prefer to dialogue rather than give whatever answers I might have. In a dialogue I take the time to think through issues once again. I think those of us who want to explore ideas carefully and also enjoy going through a process of reasoning prefer dialogue because we can see the process of reasoning unfold before us. I like an ordered sequence of steps so that I can follow themes in a systematic way. And, of course, I want to see that each step I take comes to a unity in its conclusions and something unexpected is likely to emerge. So why not join me?

Joseph: I see nothing wrong with that. I have some time. Matter of fact I would like to see what you come to with this new thing coming out of unities.

Sophron: Then, let us return to the point and proceed together like the friends that we are and see if you and I can come to an agreement together. It is worth the effort to challenge old views and, hopefully, bring us to a newer understanding because that would mean we have rid ourselves of something that we didn't know we didn't understand. Whenever that occurs then our ignorance, of course, is sacrificed.

Well, if we compare other kinds of unity and note the differences in their respective parts and how differently they function and what they bring into existence, I do think we could reach an understanding of why we can say that one kind of one is more profound than another.

Certainly some kinds of ones and unities have brought something new into existence that offers higher modes of expression than other unities.

Joseph: From something new coming into existence from unities, you now add this "higher modes of expression," but each is still a one, you know. So tell me about this "higher modes of expression." How about an example?

Sophron: You are following my trail like a true scout. Now, compare the sounds that a mob might make as they scream and shout out their demands with, say a symphonic society playing Brahms Second Piano Concerto. And then compare the Brahms with the unity of Euclid's Elements—the thirteen books of his Geometry. And with these kinds of unities doesn't each produce something different? Or compare the study of mathematics as a whole with the Brahms.

Joseph: No, I'd like to know what you believe about it.

Sophron: Shall I do that favor for you? Sure, but in turn you should favor me and answer as fully and truthfully as you can. For those capable of appreciating it, the oneness of the Brahms is actually nothing but a series of sounds; however, they have an order within which there are patterns dynamically blending into harmonies and rhythms that usher the listener into an experience of unfolding beauty. Its basic parts are sound and silence that are set against the measured movement of time, but they function much differently from those found in mechanical devices, don't they?

Joseph: And what of mathematics? What do you believe is there? Think there is a new mode of expression coming into existence there?

Sophron: You are persistent. I had hoped you would finish out the whole of it by yourself and then share it with someone. Well, the parts, or subjects, of mathematics are outside the range of sense experience since they are purely ideas set into place by its ordered premises and rules of consistency. Each field of mathematics has its own domain within which it describes and communicates through symbols and figures. As it proceeds in its ordered way it reveals patterns of symmetry and beyond that even super-symmetry by a thought process whose scope and precision are appropriate to each subject it explores. They define and bring into existence what was never seen nor thought before. With music you need players to bring into existence the music; not so for mathematics because if you can think through those symbols, you are in it. Indeed, for those capable of appreciating and understanding its oneness they can participate in her pure thought. So we can say that mathematics is man's creation, and that means discovering a rational universe of thought whose possibilities of application are open to those creative enough to see such new modes of expression that are possible.

Joseph: Yes, I see where you are going, and I have to admit that there are different kinds of ones; and while each is no less a one than the others, some can be said to bring into existence new modes of expression. Is that the point you are trying to make?

Sophron: Good questions, Joseph. That's keeping us on the right track. So then, what do you think? Should we address what it is that is common to all these different kinds of one, and discuss if a single element that runs through them all is more or less profound than those found in our examples?

Joseph: You know what? I wouldn't start counting your chickens before they hatch. I'll admit there are different kinds of ones and unities and functions, and some even turn out different products than the others, but so what? Frankly, while I like the thing you did about Brahms and mathematics, you just don't see that whatever you come to just won't fit. I believe you will do your usual trick of trying some word-game analysis of the word "profound" and pick one that fits your purpose, but it won't fly. Even if you pull it off, it won't matter anyway. I'll tell you why. What idea of God are you going to use? It's all relative to the culture, and you can't say one is better than another. In each religion and mythology you will find that each God is what it is because of the way it functions. Different way of functioning, different God—different God and you have a different religion or myth. None is better than another; frankly its all a myth.

And for God's sake, don't tell me that some ideas of god are more profound than others!

Sophron: Now, is that any way to have a dialogue? Good Heavens! I had thought you really wanted to proceed step by step, and now you are skipping all over the place. Suppose those people were listening to us: Wouldn't they be amazed at how we are conducting this talk? I do think that they would be right in believing that we wouldn't be able to give birth to anything of value the way we are going. Let's control ourselves and proceed on a moderate pace instead of rushing ahead and jumping to conclusions.

Joseph: Well, with the many ideas of God I always wonder if any are any good. You know what I mean?

Sophron: Are you saying that there is no single idea of God because there are many ideas of God, Joseph?

Joseph: I'm not sure of this, but maybe the fact that there are so many different ideas of God means that there isn't any god. Wait a minute! Maybe you can say that God is the common feature or element in all of the gods. However, it won't help, because even if all cars have something in common, that doesn't mean you'll see it drive down the road.

Sophron: Perhaps, but before you conclude that way, let me put a question to you Joseph. We call a man a carpenter in respect to what he does, do we not? But what do you say about what he is in himself apart from the way he may function? Are they not different, the thing as it is in itself and what that thing does?

Joseph: Yes, you could say that.

Sophron: So too with God: We can refer to God as the Creator and we can refer to God independent of the creating, can we not? So whenever we are asking about the functioning it is different than what is doing the functioning, correct? You do make a distinction between the man and the work done by the man, don't you? Or would you confuse the man with the table he may be making?

Joseph: So there is an idea of God that is independent of creating? So there could be many gods who might run around and play out a lot of dramas without ever being a creator, right? Like some of those Greek gods of old? So Zeus the creator creates other gods, who do no creating. Another one and many.

Sophron: Correct again, Joseph. Say, did your teacher, Eristics, ever mention Proclus? Or was he so interested in showing you how to win arguments that he failed to introduce you to the philosopher who demonstrated how philosophical principles can be personified and represented as Greek gods?

Joseph: No. Smothers never mentioned Proclus. Curious.

Sophron: He also axiomatized philosophical principles into a perfect system, and to miss out on Proclus is like leaving your daughter's marriage ceremony before finding out who married the bride.

Joseph: What's that you say? Now, that is a weird simile.

Sophron: Yes. Say, Joseph, when the carpenter is functioning as a carpenter and is applying his trade, isn't he following some plan or design?

Joseph: Sure.

Sophron: Then both the carpenter and God if they are making or creating must be following some idea?

Joseph: Yes.

Sophron: Now would you agree that the idea must itself have been created before it was used as a model for the creation?

Joseph: Yes.

Sophron: And, since that idea was the creation of God we can say it was the first creation of God. It was created prior to or before the creation of the universe, so it must have been before time, before the first day. Created out of the God itself, it must have a divine nature, and be a divine being. The idea in the mind of God being united with himself is the primal union. How shall we describe it? It must be all together, in all its perfection, an eternal idea of all that is, and it must exist as a simultaneous and eternal whole.

Joseph: That's a god if I ever heard of one. A god that created out of himself the Idea, an Idea that is divine, another god. What do you know?

Sophron: Yes, this idea in the mind of God was generated by God. Some call it the logos, the Word, or the Son of God, since it was the first creation and both is and was from that god. And the whole of it we can say is nothing other than the principles of all that later unfolds in time. For that unfoldment is a creative act, and God uses this Idea in the creation of our universe.

Joseph: So the idea in the mind of God is the highest expression of that god. You know, that is good! And that makes another kind of god, doesn't it?

Sophron: Yes, Joseph, another kind of god.

Joseph: And you say that the Word was a creative creating force?

Sophron: Have you heard it said that it was through the Word, or Logos, that all things were generated and came to be?

Joseph: Yes, I heard and read that "...what God was the Word was ...and through him all things came to be." Curious stuff. I'll have to consider it, but go on. Wait a minute! I see what you are doing. You are saying that the Word or Logos is functioning like the creator God, so itself must be a god, but it is different since it was generated by a god and generates mortal beings. Interesting.

Sophron: Since it functions as a god we can say it is another god, can't we? For this the Logos, or the Word, contains all that evolves and manifests through time. All that comes into existence and passes out of existence proceeds from this source.

Joseph: And that's another kind of god and another higher existence, right?

Sophron: Yes, indeed, and another kind of god.

Joseph: You know that I think? I'm getting a different idea of what this thing, God, is all about.

Sophron: Could be, Joseph. Now, as I recall, we said the carpenter was different from what he does, and in the same way God must be different than what he does, too. Now, if we are guided by that, we must say that what a person or thing possesses is different from that person or thing, right?

Joseph: Yes

Sophron: Then, can we say that there is a difference between the thing and its existence?

Joseph: What?

Sophron: Well, we can speak of something apart from whether or not it exists, can't we? And apart from whether or not it has being?

Joseph: I guess so. What are you getting at?

Sophron: Well, "God is" or "exists" is different from just saying "God," isn't it?

Joseph: Yes, even though that is a curious way of talking about God.

Sophron: Then the God that is responsible for all there is must itself be beyond such terms as existence and being? Yet, this God is still a One that is beyond all such terms, all qualities, and all creating?

Joseph: Ahhh, So you got your One and that is a profound one, no doubt.

Sophron: Another step.

Joseph: What?

Sophron: When we say that God is all there is, we could be referring to all that is or all that has being, couldn't we?

Joseph: This is getting a little thin, Sophron.

Sophron: Well just hold fast to something, catch your breath, and we will go on together. Consider, then, that each and every thing when taken by itself and in itself is something apart from what it may have or possess. Then, each one in all there is can be understood as a one such as we have described, and in that sense is no different from what we mean when we say God is One, which, of course, would be a pure One.

Joseph: I believe you are leaving me behind.

Sophron: Hold on for awhile longer. What if we can say that in the profoundest way of speaking what God is, as One, is a pure one, as we said? The pure One must be beyond all that exists and all that has being, yet between what is and what has being that, surely, is all that is.

Joseph: You lost me in that one. This is draining me. Wait a minute. The one that God is may not be the one that the One is? Am I making sense?

Sophron: Good question, Joseph. But if there is no difference in such ones they must be identical, and if they are identical they must be one, right? So if everything is fundamentally a one and in that sense no different than other ones, then— it is itself one and that is all there is.

Joseph: So what follows?

Sophron: Then God is itself One and all there is. And if God is all there is, then each and everything is a one, then there are only a ones, right?

Joseph: I guess so.

Sophron: Yes, which is simultaneously everywhere and throughout all time without the slightest difference.

Joseph: I do think that point was lost on me.

Sophron: If not the slightest difference then both space and time are irrelevant to the One. Curious isn't it that we can proceed through a mystery as profound as this?

Joseph: What? Aren't you seeing all this as we were going?

Sophron: I would like to think I know where I'm going, but it just occurred to me that we haven't even raised the question of how we must be to be a one, you know, like the One we say God is? For surely if God

BIRTHING A PRAYER 87

is all there is, and God is One, we should know how to be to be that. I do believe I goofed there, and you didn't even stop me.

Joseph: How?

Sophron: Did I say we have to learn to be that which is truly one? I do think we said something like that. But if we are going to be like that, we would have to become like that and be like that; yet we said that if anything does anything it would be different from what it is in itself. Didn't we say something like that? Are you getting up to leave, Joseph?

Joseph: Yes, I just realized I may be late for a meeting. I enjoyed our talk.

Sophron: But, wait. Consider, do we have to be anything to be one? What do we have to do to be one if we are one?

Joseph: I think I have to leave, but before I do would you say that there are some people around here who enjoy going into that question?

Sophron: Enjoy? Well, I think we know that some people do say that joy is a sign of the presence of God, and giving up your ignorance is a sure sign of entering that presence.

Joseph: What? That's a curious expression. I thought I heard it somewhere, but when you say it, it sounds different. Something about it that I like. What do you mean by "giving up your ignorance"?

Sophron: I don't know if I can explain it, but if you wait for a few minutes before leaving I may be able to put a few questions to you that might make it clearer.

Joseph: Go ahead, Sophron.

Sophron: Say, Joseph, if you really wanted to become clear about what we have said, would you have to go over it? Now, if you did take that challenge and went over it again and again, I would imagine that in the end you would understand this as much as anyone could be brought to understand it. The reason I say this is because I wonder if you would tell me what it would do to you to do this? I think I should be able to say this in a less cumbersome way. You can choose to remain as you are without going into it any deeper. You know that?

Joseph: Yeah, I think I'm following. I'd say for me to go carefully over this, to consider each of the points, and to see them all clearly would make me do something I've not done for awhile. I would have to be more sure of myself and the way I think. Maybe I would be better for it and maybe not.

Sophron: So you have to decide whether or not to give up your ignorance?

Joseph: That's a crazy way to put it. Oh, I see your point, because if I were to really make myself understand this I would be giving up all the ways that I call me.

Sophron: So to give up your ignorance would be a kind of sacrifice, wouldn't it? Like you would be laying aside an old way of being and stepping into an unknown and more significant way of being, wouldn't you? Is it not possible that kind of sacrifice might make you a more interesting person, Joseph?

Joseph: A more interesting one, Sophron? Now that was making a point that was profound. Never heard that idea of sacrifice. I believe it would not be an easy thing to give up.

Sophron: That's true. In the old days when someone needed to be helped or delivered from their ignorance, they called on philosophical midwives because those who can assist another in bringing to birth what they were long pregnant with were midwives.

Joseph: One kind of midwife births children, another the ideas that you need help delivering. Those who help birth ideas are taught to recognize those ideas that should see the light of day, and those not. Say, Sophron, where did you hear about this idea of prayer?

Sophron: It is an old idea that is returning. According to an old Greek story there was a god, Prometheus, and it was he who brought the arts down from the heavens so that man could survive not as an animal but as Man. He taught man how to sacrifice to the gods, and it is this idea that takes on a new name today: prayer.

Joseph: Where do they do these kinds of things?

Sophron: Where people come together to discover the furthermost reach of the mind. It is all part of the Platonic tradition. What Parmenides, Plato, Plotinus, and Proclus developed may be coming back. Did you know that the founder of the Church of Religious Science frequently cites Plato and Plotinus?

Joseph: Really? Are you thinking that it may take a Platonic direction? Now, that is really interesting. I don't even know what that would mean.

Sophron: Actually, Joseph, there is and there isn't a Platonic tradition. Let me explain. Whoever accepts the idea that we can participate in the divine and find in such experiences the terms and categories for organizing one's philosophy, then they are rational. Some people call that Platonic, but it is really recognizing that the mind and spirit, the reach of the intellect, and seeking the divine through devotion are one. And that the conditions for understanding are the same as those for loving, so that the highest aspirations of man can be united into one, and find in the one what is the highest good. As for the destiny of this or that church, I think that each seeks its own path consistent with its highest vision, and where that ends neither I nor you can guess.

Joseph: Well, that's enough for me.

Sophron: Where are you going?

Joseph: I guess it follows that if you decide to play this noblest game you have a job to do on yourself. You know that's a lot of work! I'm going to take a walk—need time to think about this.

Being, the One
a philosophical dialogue

Pierre Grimes

Original 1976 publication with Cover Design by Rod Wallbank.

Being, The One: Author's Introduction

This dialogue was written to provide a context within which the thought of Parmenides could be explored. It was designed both to present the kinds of reflections and questions that always seem to attend discussions of philosophical monism, as well as an approach to help overcome some of those inevitable difficulties which oftentimes cause perplexity when dealing with Parmenidean thought. The midpoint of this dialogue-play contains a new translation of the poem of Parmenides.

Parmenides founded a school of philosophy at Elea in Italy about 540 B.C.; however there is much uncertainty as to the exact date. In his youth Parmenides was said to have studied with Xenophanes, and while there is much obscurity concerning his personal life, we do know that he has been honored and held in the highest esteem by Plato and many other philosophers, especially those who have pursued a metaphysical monism.

Parmenides was among the earliest philosophers to develop a systematic approach to reach the nature of Reality by pure reason, and the first to adhere to the principles of logical coherence and consistency.

The poem of Parmenides is both a dramatic masterpiece and a profound statement of his own vision of Reality. It is sometimes thought that visionary experiences are irrational or supernatural, but today more people are coming to realize that such experiences can also be a supremely rational condition of man's mind, the content of which can be explored through reason. The poem itself contains no mystery, salvation, or worship; thus its religious significance may not be apparent to those whose contact with religion is based exclusively on devotional Christianity; but when explored among other experiences of a similar nature their similarities and differences emerge, revealing Parmenides' vision to be among the most profound.

The existence of a philosophy reaching as far back as 540 B.C. – which is as early as man's recorded history—to the present day, and appearing in many diverse cultures yet containing a similar message throughout, is the claim of a philosophia perennis, Perennial Philosophy; the philosophy that adheres to reason and culminates in a vision of the Oneness of ultimate reality. In the history of speculative thought the role of these thinkers has had a profound effect and has shaped the cultural development of civilizations. A study of such men and their works would offer an opportunity to explore the flower of human thought and would certainly include among its members such men as Parmenides, Melissus, Plato, Plotinus, Damascius, Al Farabi, Ibn Rushd, Suhrawardi, Confucius, LaoTzu, Shankaracharya, Guadapada, Nargajuna, Chandrikirti, Bassui, Dogen, B.F. Bradley, and the writings of the Surangama Sutra, Lankavatara Sutra, and the Negative Theology of PseudoDionysius.

The poem itself contains many puzzles for scholars, one of which is the order to the parts of the poem. The many parts that make up the whole were found in the writings of Hellenistic and Christian authors and hence are called fragments. The question of their proper order in the poem has not been settled with any finality; in any case the order of the fragments used in our translation is that of Herman Diels.

The translation of the poem of Parmenides was artfully done by William Uzgalis, a man who has sought to comprehend monistic philosophy for some years and, therefore, is particularly suited for the translation.

An earlier version of the dialogue was video-taped at Golden West College in Huntington Beach, California by a group of philosophers turned actors, The Platonic Players. The music composed for this occasion by Al Maitland added to its success. Changes have been made in this play, primarily to serve the needs of students and those to whom an exploration into the question of the One is an introduction into Hellenistic thought.

The original play, The One, served a different purpose than this present work, and since extensive changes have been made, including much philosophical reflection, the title has been changed from *The One* to *Being, The One*.

An Invitation

This dialogue and translation of the poem of Parmenides preserves in some way our accumulated thought on the mystery of the One. However, it is not meant to be final, but marks in some way where we are. I use the term "we" purposely, because thought, in so far as it is in dialogue, is both a sharing and, when testing one's own thought, a solitary quest in the company of rational men. Therefore, enter into the dialogue about the nature of the one, or Reality, and become a participant in an enquiry that knows neither a boundary of time nor place; and discover, if you can, why it has gone on for so long and commanded the attention of so many of the world's great men.

List of Characters:

EROTIMA, A PRIESTESS

GLAUCON, A FRIEND OF PHILOLAUS

PHILOLAUS, A FRIEND OF PARMENIDES

PARMENIDES

THE GODDESS

Being, The One

A Philosophical Dialogue

with

Parmenides' Poem

Translated by William Uzgalis

Scene 1:

Erotima, a priestess from Pydna, is relating a story to a group of men and women. The atmosphere is intense, yet relaxed. The tone is that of a serious discussion.

Erotima: You have invited me to tell of my journey to Athens, but the journey itself was uneventful, so let me relate what I found to be of significance, for what was said there and the discussions that followed were of importance. They absorbed me fully and it continues to challenge me each time I tell this story. However, before I begin, I should first say that after that day in Athens I sought out each of the participants and they recalled what was said and I went over it many times in order to be sure my account left out nothing of value.

Well, after leaving our home in Pydna, on the slopes of Mount Olympus, and traveling south, we finally reached Athens and met Glaucon, Ariston's son, in the marketplace. He greeted us warmly and asked us the reason for our visit. I remarked that we had sought him out to find out if he could give us a full account of the visit of Parmenides of Elea, or if he could not, to refer us to someone who could. I went on to say, that while we have some interest in philosophy, we at Pydna are too close to other things, and few of our fellows ever journey to Athens to get an accurate report of the event, and it appears also that you Athenians sometimes forget your obligation to inform us about what is being said and done in your city.

Scene 2:

Erotima's recollection of her dialogue with Glaucon.

Glaucon: Then you have heard of the journey of Parmenides, Erotima?

Erotima: Oh, yes, we did hear of it, but hadn't realized its importance until Ion of Ephesus' recent studies of Hesiod and Archilochus acquainted us with its possibilities.

Glaucon: I'll tell you what you want to know, but first you must tell me what Ion said he saw, for I am more than curious to know what could have moved you to reconsider it. Surely that would be a fair exchange, for it has been some years since it was first discussed, and while many have heard and some discuss it, only a few of the most dedicated still seriously deal with it.

Erotima: True, but as you no doubt have heard, Ion once thought of himself as a master of reciting until he had a certain discussion and was forced to admit that a master of an art must not be content knowing only a part of his art, even when it is the best and most divine part. And, he saw too that the pretense of knowing is not worth the effort it entails, even when one can claim divine inspiration. As a result, Ion said he recognized that he must understand what all the good poets say, learn their meaning thoroughly, and be the interpreter of the poets' mind to the audience. So you see he is no longer content with mastering what is considered the most divine scripture, Homer. Since that time he and his reciting have changed remarkably, and recently he has been demonstrating that many of the references in the vision of Parmenides are directly related to the sacred writings of Homer, Hesiod, and others.

After pondering and questioning deeply, he now advances the opinion that Parmenides might be saying something of deep significance, either in competition with these divine poets, or, and this is what we find most curious, that he is seeking to go beyond them. Now, as you know, we like to think of ourselves as close to what matters most to men and gods, yet not having heard any more of this, we were forced to surmise and guess at the rest, because you see Ion admits that while he knows something about the whole, he will only discourse upon the section he feels he has mastered, and that section is called the Journey.

Glaucon: I see the significance of that story about Ion, so come, you can't stop there with your account. What is it about this possibility that seems so important to you now? And tell me, in what part did you see or intuit the whole? And what kind of a whole is it that you think you have glimpsed?

Erotima: I think you want to test us to see what we have discovered from the fragments we found. All right then, we first discussed what we had been able to piece together from the report of Ion's and the accounts of others, as well as what we added or guessed, and it seemed that, according to Ion, Parmenides might be saying that Being is above the gods, or what is stranger yet, that the gods themselves are One. Further it seemed he could also be saying that the many things are, in fact, One. However, we thought that such a belief, which runs counter to all that we know to be true, might properly be a subject for humor rather than philosophy; for surely, the gods are many, not One, and as we all know, the animals around us and all the plants and trees, including any man-made thing, if each a One, then taken together they constitute a many, not a one. However, as you know, Ion is very convincing and insisted that such a teaching clothed in such images from Homer and Hesiod should not be dismissed lightly, and just might contain more of a challenge and an opportunity than we realized.
Glaucon: Yes it would be a challenge, but "an opportunity"? An opportunity for what?

Erotima: To see what philosophers are exploring and saying.

Glaucon: I knew you were once seriously interested in philosophy, but I thought after you became a priestess you no longer were concerned with philosophy.

Erotima: That is true, but I have returned to it in a new way recently.

Glaucon: Then tell me, Erotima, what has reawakened your interest in philosophy, especially in the kind of challenge found in Parmenidean thought? For it has been some time since you showed any interest in such thought. I have heard that you are encountering some difficulty in Pydna with the teachings of Hostanes, the Archimagus, the one who both accompanied and spoke for the Great King of the Persians, Xerxes, in his invasion of our lands. Could it be that you hope to discover some way out of your troubles through the philosophy of Parmenides?

Erotima: It would be better if you would call him Hostanes the despoiler of mankind or the Plague-carrier. We dealt with Darius, then his son Xerxes; they sought to annihilate us, their armies tried to destroy our lands, they desecrated our temples and holy places, but their mighty power conceals a spirit of carnage and their words are devious, designed by guile to undermine our people's trust in the manifestation of the gods. Their armies have been repelled, the debris they left as they scattered homeward is visible proof of our victory, but Hostanes' words have started a new struggle, a new battle fought in the minds of our people.

Glaucon: I am not as informed about his teachings as, perhaps, I should be, but from what I have heard his teachings are so far removed from what I would call intelligible that I, as well as others, have ignored them. Yet, from what you say, you see a greater threat than I had imagined. What have you found in their words that is so threatening?

Erotima: They hold that man plays a vital role in a cosmic drama. They believe that the universe is a battle ground between the forces of good and evil. Man, they feel, is called upon to make his choice in this struggle not by words, but by his deeds. This vast battle is to continue until evil is utterly destroyed; after this victory they expect a resurrection, a final judgment and, afterwards, a universal peace will follow for believers, but the followers of evil will plunge straight into hell. All their followers must believe this to be true. They must join in annihilating the worship of all other gods and, therefore, they are expected to serve as soldiers in a battle between light and darkness. They honor belief and reject all that opposes their belief, regarding it as evil.

Glaucon: For myself, I would like to explore how a person can believe all that. I would like to know what happens to them if they can believe it, and how they handle their conflict with reason when they do believe it. But let me put that aside for later discussions and ask you what you and your friends at Delos and Dodona see in this belief that is dangerous to we Hellenics.

Erotima: We clearly see their belief goes through a series of stages; at first the belief is said to be a war in Heaven between spirits of good and evil; then it becomes a personal conflict within man himself; after that it is fought against other men; and finally, if they are successful, they wage war against their neighboring states. When they triumph they usher in a dark age for all under their domain because they assign evil to others, condemn all other beliefs, and seek to annihilate those who oppose them.

Glaucon: Then our victory at Marathon and Salamis should have taught them that their god had failed.

Erotima: No, they see it as merely one battle in a long protracted war in which their god will ultimately triumph.

Glaucon: Yes, I understand that part of their belief, but didn't the disaster they suffered in those battles have any force or impact upon the believers?

Erotima: No, because neither experience nor reason can sway their belief.

Glaucon: I am puzzled by that because I would imagine that they would soon see the character and form of their deity is, in truth, merely that of a war lord or warrior who needs an army of mortals to win his divine battle; and while they acknowledge the war is a long struggle, they can't or don't question the wisdom of the strategy or the general's competence. Such a people do not fully comprehend the nature of form and its meaning, nor that in form itself lies a truer reality.

Erotima: I would like to learn more about this idea of form, is it Parmenidean?

Glaucon: Yes, and I don't have to be an oracle to tell that you will find Parmenides' thought a real challenge. I think you should hear it from those who continue to explore his thought, and of course, I will go along with you. I was not present when Parmenides' Poem was first delivered but heard it some years later from others who were fortunate enough to have been there at the time. Perhaps we should journey to Melite to hear it from Pythodorus' old friend, Philolaus, for there are times when I see his vision as a puzzle ensconced within a riddle and therefore I would find it to my advantage to hear it again.

Erotima: You know, it is not this Zoroastrian belief alone that concerns me, for this whole thing about Parmenides I find puzzling. Consider this: you know he expresses himself in the same style and uses the same images as are found in the divinely inspired Homer, yet he is a philosopher, not a poet. However, in expressing himself in this way, would you not think his intention is to give his philosophy the mark and character of sacred scripture? Does he seek to go beyond what is the belief of our fathers; the very belief that has inspired our people to become one and share in the strength of the Hellenic unity? Is he another threat? Or does he think he can strengthen us in our struggle against this new barbarism?

Glaucon: That's even more reason to hear it from Philolaus. Let us walk there together and discuss some of the possible consequences of all this.

Erotima resumes her story.

Erotima: When we arrived in Melite and found Philolaus, we were surprised to find that he was quick to discover the purpose of our visit and why it seemed so important to us. He invited us into his home, and after his attendants made us comfortable and offered us wine, he told us the whole story. He started by recalling that when he was a young man he was always anxious to hear any discussion dealing with the pursuit of philosophy, and therefore seized the opportunity to meet with others when he heard that Parmenides was going to be in Ceramicus during the Great Panathenaia, at the elder Pythodorus' home.

Scene 3:

Erotima's recollection continues. The setting is a small gathering at Philolaus' home.

Philolaus: You are asking of me what I most want to give, so let me first offer thanks to whatever may be for your request. I am always ready to discuss philosophy, because by such reflections one returns to our source, much like the wandering moon looking to the sun's rays. In those early days philosophy was explored through many discussions and dialogues; we were able to see it unfold among many of us but it was Parmenides who seemed to be in some strange way closer than any of us to Philosophy itself. In those days we were drawn to philosophy because of him, for when you saw Parmenides it was terribly difficult not to try to become like him, a philosopher. In exploring an idea with him you could see your own conflicts with reason emerge. It was as if his method became a mirror in which, sooner or later, you either had to see yourself or find his company too difficult to bear. Indeed, one of the poets who knew him well was fond of saying:

"Parmenides, a gift of the gods, became a hymn to the gods. Through him they saw themselves in their own divine radiance."

Well, you must understand that prior to hearing Parmenides' account we heard reports of it from travelers from Elea, especially a certain Pythagorean named Ameinias, son of Diochaitas, and it caused a few of us to shake our heads in puzzlement and wonder. Since it was not unusual for us to come together to discuss matters of importance, we began to deal with the consequences of, what we believed, were his views. All our talk kept turning around one central point, much like a wheel on its nave, but where we were going we didn't know. We explored with each other the possibility that if there is something unchanging it must not be in the world we experience since everything about us is changing, and even if it did exist it couldn't have any relationship with what we encounter. Everything changes, everything is a manyness. If only the unchanging One or Being exists then our experience of a manyness must be a dream, a madness which can't even exist, and therefore must be non-being.

On the other hand we were aware that in studying our experiences, seeing how things behave and trying to determine recurrent patterns, we come to see order and the intelligibility behind things. But if only the unchanging One or Being exists, all this must also be the fabric of our illusion, and so too love, thought, and reason; but this could not be since we knew Parmenides would never turn away from things of the mind. Yet if what we heard was true it seemed to us that all this must be relegated to the many, to appearance, and so to unreality. We were somewhat astonished by our conclusion, because the One itself, then, seemed barren and peripheral to all that we sought so earnestly in philosophy. It seemed Parmenides must be praising a thing only a stone could find kinship with. It seemed that to agree with Parmenides meant sacrificing reason, thought, and all that we Hellenics so loved. If we were to deny those things we would have betrayed the very things that originally had drawn us into philosophy. How could we deny what separated us from the barbarians? We felt we had been robbed by the very sentinel and guardian we had appointed to protect us and so we felt we may have reached a truth, but in doing so we had lost both the meaning and significance that seemed so vital to us all. The more we dwelt on this, the more it seemed that the many was more praiseworthy and to be honored than the One, which now appeared austere and barren.

We knew Parmenides knew but we didn't know what he knew nor even how he knew. It was often said Parmenides had a vision, but none of us had directly heard it. We thought that if we could urge him to relate it to us, it might provide us with the clues to what we so desperately sought to understand and know. We were aware that visions are private, personal affairs, yet we felt that if we could show our own seriousness and sincerity to be no less than his own he would help us. Therefore we decided to invite him to tell of his vision and then after we would discuss it among ourselves and probe it for its meaning. We wanted to understand his vision, to see in it all its dimensions, thereby sharing in the vision, which, by reflection, we hoped would shape our own.

Thus, we asked him to tell his vision without adding one word either of explanation or of commentary, for we wanted it as close to its original form as possible. He agreed. And so, on that day, without one word of introduction, after lighting a sacrificial fire to Apollo, he turned to us, remained silent for a few moments and recalled his vision.

Scene 4:

Parmenides and the Goddess.

Parmenides' Poem

1. The mares which bear me, reaching as far as the heart could desire, escorted me, when they went, guiding me, on to the much fabled way of the divinity, which bears the man who knows throughout every city; on it I bore myself, for on it the very wise horses conveyed me, galloping with the chariot, while maidens led the way. The axle blazing in the nave let loose a piping hum (for it was urged round by a whirling wheel on either side), when the hand maidens of the Sun, throwing back their veils from off their faces with their hands, left the Halls of Night, and hastened to convey

me into the light. There are the gates of the ways of both Night and Day, and they have an embracing lintel and a marble threshold; they are aeithereal but are closed by great doors; and much laboring righteousness holds their alternating latches. The maidens speaking gently, paying attention to every detail, persuaded her, so that she quickly threw back the fastened bolt from the gates; the opening of the gates made a wide expanse, revealing the door posts wrought of bronze, the hinges held with revolving bolts in their hollow parts and fastened with spikes; at once the maidens guide the chariot and horses straight through them on the high road. And the goddess greeted me graciously, she grasped my right hand with her hand, and she spoke words in this wise and addressed me: "Youth, linked with immortal charioteers and the mares which bear you to our halls, welcome, since no evil fate, but Righteousness and Order sent you forth on this road (which is far from the path of men). It is right for you to learn all things, both the calm heart of well-rounded truth and the opinions of mortals among which there is no persuasive truth. In the same way, you will learn these things also, how the appearances rightfully appear to be, all being in the midst of each.

2. Come now, I will tell you, and you after listening to the fateful story carry it away; these are the only roads of inquiry for thought; the one both that it is and cannot not be, this is the road of Persuasion (for it attends upon Truth), while the other both that it is not, and that not being rightfully is. This path I declare to be without tidings, for neither can you know not being (for it is impossible) nor can you speak it.

3. For it is the same thing both to think and to be.

4. Gaze at things which are far away yet securely present to mind. For one will not cut off being from clinging to being. For neither does it wholly scatter itself everywhere throughout the universe nor combine together.

5. It is inseparable from me where I shall begin, for I shall return back there again.

6. Both saying and thinking that being is is right, for to be is, while nothing is not; I bid you ponder these things. From this first road of inquiry I hold you back, but next from this one, on which mor-

tals knowing nothing, wander, two headed; for helplessness guides the wandering mind in their hearts; there are crowds of them without judgement borne violently about both deaf and blind, amazed, by whom to be and not to be are thought to be the same and not the same, it is the backwards turning road of all things.

7. Never shall this be demonstrated, that not being is; but from this road of inquiry hold back your thought. Nor let habit force you down that much experienced road, guiding your aimless eye and echoing ear and tongue, but judge by reason this much contested refutation spoken by me.

8. There remains then but one tale of the road; Is; there are very many signs upon this road, that being is unborn and imperishable, complete, unique, and both calm and perfect; nor was it once nor will be in the future, since it is now, altogether, one, embracing; for what birth will you seek out for it? Whence and in what way did it grow? Nor will I allow you either to say or think it came from not being. For it is unsayable and unthinkable that not being is. What thing would stir it up to grow, starting from not being, sooner rather than later? Thus either to be rightfully is, altogether; or it is not. The strength of persuasion will not allow anything ever to come from being besides itself, nor is it proper for Righteousness to loosen the fetters on being born and dying, but holds them; the decision concerning these things is in the following terms; is or is not; one has decided for oneself, therefore, to allow this road to be unthought of and unnamed (for it is not the true road), so that the other is the true and genuine road. How could being be in the future? How could it be born? For if it was or will be at some time, it is not, thus birth and unheard of death are extinguished. Nor is it distinguishable within itself, since it is all the same, not more here nor less there, which might prevent it from embracing, but it is all full of being. Thus, it is all embracing. For being clings to being. But motionless in the limits of great bonds it is without start or pause, since birth and death were driven very far away, while true persuasion drove them off. The same both remains in the same and reposes by itself, and so it remains there securely; for mighty Necessity holds it in the bonds of limit, for it holds it back all around, for on account of Order, being is not unlimited; it is without lack, for it would need everything. Both thinking and that on account of

which there is thought are the same. For you will not find thinking without being, in what is uttered; for nothing either is or will be except being, since Fate bound it whole and immovable; so, with respect to this thing have all names which mortals established believing to be true, been spoken, coming to be and perishing, being and not being, and both change of place and exchange of bright color. But since there is an outermost limit, it is completed, like on all sides the shape of a well rounded sphere, it is evenly balanced from the center in all directions; for it is not rightfully somewhat greater nor somewhat smaller here rather than there. For neither is there not being, which might prevent it from reaching the same, nor is it possible that being is more than being here and less than it there, since it is all unbreakable, for it is equal on all sides, it reaches out equally in limits. At this point I cease my persuasive account and thought about truth; but learn from this the opinions of mortals, hearing the deceptive order of my words. For they decided to name two thought forms (morphe), the unity of which rightfully is not named - in this they have wandered - for they have distinguished opposites and assumed that they are different in form (demas) and signs from one another, on the one hand the aethereal light of flame, being gentle and very rarefied, the same with itself in every way, but not the same with the other, and that other is, in itself, the opposite, dark night, close and heavy in form (demas). I tell you the whole probable arrangement of the universe so that no opinion of mortals will ever surpass you.

9. But when all things were named light and night and these in accordance with their powers both for these and those, everything is full of light and of invisible night together, since there is nothing which does not belong to either.

10. You will know the aeithereal nature and all the signs of the aeither and the invisible works of the pure holy torch of the sun and whence they came into being, and you will learn both the nature and the wandering works of the round eyed moon, you will learn of the all embracing sky and whence it grew, and how Necessity guided it and fettered it to hold the limit of the stars.

11. ...how earth and sun and moon both the inseparable aeither and the milky way, the outermost olympus, and the burning power of the stars were stirred up to come into being.

12. For the narrower rings are filled with pure fire while those that come after them are filled with night while a share of light is let loose among them; and in their midst is the goddess who steers all things everywhere. For she rules over love and hateful birth sending female to mingle with male, and again, male to mingle with female.

13. The very first of all gods she contrived Eros.

14. Shining by night with borrowed light wandering around the earth.

15. Always looking towards the sun's rays.

16. For each time the mixture of the much wandering limbs holds fast, in this way mind comes to man; for it is the same for all men and for each what the ordering power of the body thinks. For the excess is thought.

17. On the right boys, on the left girls.

18. When woman and man mix the seeds of love together, the power forming from opposite blood in the veins, by preserving proper proportion shapes a well formed body. Now if the powers fight, when the seeds are mixed, they will torment the growing embryo by the conflict of double seed.

19. So, let me tell you, according to belief, these things were born and now are and afterwards, having grown, they will perish, for each men have established a distinctive name.

Scene 5:

The dialogue between Philolaus, Erotima and Glaucon resumes after Parmenides' account.

Philolaus: This, then, is the vision of Parmenides, but what is more remarkable is that he followed the Goddess' words and seemed to grow deeper into the vision until his death in the sixty-ninth Olympiad.

Erotima: What do you mean when you say he grew into the vision?

Philolaus: The Journey was a vision, it caused his vision to deepen, but it was not what most, or even you, would regard as a divine vision.

Erotima: I am not following you, what do you mean?

Philolaus: Would you call a vision an event brought about by something other than ourselves, as from the divine?

Erotima: Of course.

Philolaus: And if one had several such visions or experiences would you not call that man fortunate indeed and at the same time wonder if he may not have had some role in the occurrence himself?

Glaucon: Yes, I would wonder about that.

Philolaus: But if you were to discover that what you are calling a vision is a continuous state of mind, not something a man can go in and out of, but as it were, part of his very being, would you still call it a vision?

Glaucon: No, I don't think I would, but how does this apply to his account of the Journey?

Philolaus: Consider the time sense of the Journey of Parmenides, does he not describe it as having occurred in the past, yet extending, without any sense of having been completed or finished, to the present?

Glaucon: I'm not sure.

Philolaus: Perhaps I can make it clearer. Consider the words of Parmenides, doesn't he say: "the mares which bear me?" Well, those words express an action that continues, for indeed the mares continue to bear him and clearly it would be a mistake to assume it was completed or finished, rather it has the force of continuing into the present an action initiated earlier. Now, considering that the Journey describes the nature of the experience, then it would follow that a continuous state must be a state of mind rather than a vision, or even a repeated vision, because it is in the nature of a vision that it must have a beginning and an end, something one can go in and out of; however, a continued state of mind should be called a clear waking vision in which realities are simply present to the mind. For ease in our discussion we can continue to call it a vision, even a repeated vision, so long as you remember its proper meaning when you reflect upon it later.

Erotima: Do you mean it became his own way of seeing?

Philolaus: Yes.

Erotima: What effect did all this have upon you and your friends?

Philolaus: Well, we, those of us nearest to him, have continued to this day to ponder what was revealed, or made clear, to him. Some of the others were tempted to either simply believe the truths revealed to him, or to reject it all, believing it false, but we regard belief in any form as chaining the spirit of the mind to the hard, barren rocks of the earth, and rather than live out a self-inflicted punishment, we continually seek to mature our own vision, to give flight to that part of us which seeks higher unities, not unlike that chariot ride that soared into the light of Reality. So, you will find us questioning, discussing, and reflecting on his words and urging others to do the same, thinking it the better part of a man's life to pursue such reflections.

Glaucon: I can see why you would reject beliefs but I never could understand why you favor questions rather than answers; surely of the two, answers are superior to questions, as knowing is to not-knowing. What possible importance do you see in continuing the state of not-knowing?

Philolaus: You think it strange that we treasure questions more than answers perhaps because you are not aware that when these questions are pursued with the utmost sincerity one discovers that out of the silence of the moment emerges a mode of seeing with the mind alone ... while answers have a different source, for they are past beliefs returning to be put into service again; habit replaces the vision and so we are fettered to the past and become like the mad prisoner who praises his chains and finds security in his prison.

When you or I accept an answer it is because it fits easily into beliefs we regard as truths and so it gives an appearance of truth; it has the feel of a unity but its parts are joined together without thought and understanding. This is far different from the true unity that can be encountered beyond the level of belief, where we see and gaze at things distant yet present to the mind and experience in simplicity a unity that binds and embraces both itself and the things it relates, for in that experience our understanding reaches a more lofty level.

You know, you seem to favor answers which keep you from a state of being numbed by not-knowing, a trait which could make a man a Sophist. Thus, let me urge you to watch yourself carefully, to become aware of what happens when you accept an answer, even mine, and see whether in accepting it you are paying homage not to the divinity, but to a cruel authority who could never become a beloved king. Should you wish to regain your lost sovereignty ... it is difficult, yet one way is to accept only answers which permit even grander questions, in the way a scaffold is used in the construction of a temple, or an answer might become a step in a series of steps climbing to higher questions. Recall Parmenides says "one must decide for oneself," which means we must value our doubts and puzzles and most sincerely struggle with our own questions. It is really the answer that is strange, for an answer may prematurely end the life of a question, preventing it from reaching its full flowering. Thus you will find that we try to avoid believing, and prefer to question even the words of Parmenides as seriously as we must our own or else we know we will remain strangers to what we most desire to see and partake of ourselves. We start with Parmenides' vision, reason our way to the One, and then force ourselves to turn about and ask why the universe appears as many, as imperfect, when our reason tells us it "simply is," or is One.

Our challenge is to remain with the conclusion of reason while facing fully the evidence of our everyday experience, which seems so compelling, leading us to the belief that "the many is" and "the One is not." The questions force us to doubt what we formerly felt was so true and certain. Thus, by taking the question one accepts the invitation to refute one's own answer. This way of proceeding builds our confidence in reason and intelligence and slowly breaks our habit of relying on the eyes, ears, and all the senses for the truth about reality.

Pursuing these questions may appear as a madness, but it may not be as mad as believing the many to be real and the One illusion. This then is our life, a life dedicated to the One and questioning "the many."

Glaucon: It may be as you say, I often recall you saying that there is no fundamental conspiracy, no deception, because appearances provide us with a glimpse of reality. I think I see more into this than before, but I feel I have not yet grasped it as I wish I could. For myself, I find nothing difficult in grouping order and reason together, but in Parmenides' poem the Goddess frequently mentions embracing, being clinging together, and love. How can love and reason be reconciled into a unity, or one? Certainly love is the most irrational of things.

Philolaus: It may be that your belief about reason is at the root of all this; try another approach. Consider both reason and love in their best moments, not when they are mixed and impure. Such times when each seems to show itself best, then ask yourself what kinds of things, what kinds of moods and feelings must be present for each to function ... at its best? Then see how much of each is hidden, as if in disguise, in the other. If these can be reconciled then in two you can see one.

Glaucon: That is interesting. I'll try to puzzle it out and if I find a oneness out of those two then I'll be amazed. Could that be for other things as well? If so, then ... we produce the many? Could it really be that in making or discovering differences we bring into existence our entire familiar world? I always find this very difficult to accept because that possibility requires that I must deny my experience of difference. And how can I do that when my experience so clearly demonstrates the existence of differences and most especially between love and reason? If I deny difference is real I would have to deny that I actually am experiencing, and that is to me, just impossible to do.

Philolaus: Does the Goddess reject perception and experience, or our way of judging these things? For there is no problem in distinguishing opposites such as darkness and light, only in assuming that they are different in form and sign from one another.

Glaucon: When Erotima and I were walking to your house we were discussing this very problem of the difference between "morphe" and "demas," or form and in form, and even *though* I have heard and reflected upon it before I had some difficulty making it clear to her, so I would find it both to my advantage, as well as to Erotima's, to review it with you now.

Philolaus: Erotima, do you regard all things that have form different from what has no form, and that having form means that there is some unity and organizing principle present, while that without form is said to lack these qualities?

Erotima: Yes.

Philolaus: And, when some people distinguish light from darkness, and say the spirit in each is opposite to the other, do they not confuse the form a thing has with the spirit they believe is *in* the form?

Erotima: Yes, I can see that point.

Philolaus: And when they call one "gentle" and the other "close," are they not adding to each signs or qualities they believe are *in* the form, and not the form we see and distinguish?

Erotima: True, and I can see that they can easily move from that to calling one good and beneficent, and the other evil and sinister.

Philolaus: Yes, and would it not be a simple step, in such thinking, to call them opposed or enemies at war with one another?

Erotima: Yes, I see what you mean.

Philolaus: Yet all this can only be true if the indwelling spirit that organizes and gives unity to all things can be said to be opposed to itself simply because it enters into opposite forms, such as light and dark.

Erotima: But that is their belief!

Philolaus: So they cover their ignorance with the word belief, without wondering if it is even believable, for surely some things are unbelievable.

Erotima: Then when they place their deity apart from the intelligible that recurs in all forms they have lost all contact with what is meaningful.

Philolaus: Quite true, only add another thing, for they also lose the opportunity to discover the nature of the divine that holds these forms together.

Erotima: So our natural world seems to be at war when we attribute, in form and sign, such radical differences. I think I recall Homer's use of "demas," but I'm not sure how it applies to "in form."

Philolaus: Recall in the Iliad when it is said: "so fought they like unto blazing fire;" as the blazing fire is a "demas" to express the nature or spirit of fighting men, so in Parmenides, close and heavy is a "demas" to express the nature of a night without luminaries - or as it is sometimes described, an obscure night. So a "demas" is a simile used to express more dramatically an inner form or spirit inherent *in* any form. However, they ignore the simile and believe it literally; a simple mistake that has serious consequences on all who come in contact with them.

Glaucon: But those who believe this do attract men who seek to battle evil and in that their belief certainly seems to make them less evil and so better men.

Philolaus: Better in what sense?

Glaucon: I have heard that they are urged to perform many good deeds and to speak the truth.

Philolaus: Are they brave because they fear a greater evil?

Erotima: Yes, they fear plunging directly into hell if they are evil or fail to obey the commands of Zoroaster and his priests.

Philolaus: Then they appear good and do good deeds out of fear?

Erotima: Yes, out of fear.

Philolaus: Are not those who are moved to act out of fear called cowards?

Erotima: Why yes, that is true.

Philolaus: Then they only appear to be good and righteous, since the good they do is out of cowardice and fear of hell. They can hardly be called good, for the actions of those who are good must spring from themselves, not from fear.

Erotima: Yes, it seems they only appear good and are not good. I see that now, but considering what you said before are we not now saying that in respect to themselves, or *in* form, they differ, having different spirits?

Philolaus: No, because they themselves have not changed. They are still ignorant of what it is to be a man.

Erotima: But how can we understand that what is in form is not different, because the visible differences are so real?

Philolaus: Consider it in this way, Erotima. If all the objects in a man's home are made of potter's clay, then are they not all made of the same clay? Yet we can distinguish one object from another, but in respect to the basic underlying material is there any difference? For fundamentally they are all made from the same clay, are they not?

Glaucon: Potter's clay! I have heard that before, Erotima, and my question Philolaus knows so well, even as I do his next answer. How are you going to be sure it's all the same, Philolaus, as in the case of the clay, and I believe your answer is going to be, "that's the need for the vision of Being." No, I would rather go a different way because it seems to me that all this comes down to the presumed difference between distinguishing and judging difference. If that's correct, then we are simply making a mistake, and since that may be likely, we need only ask: "How can we correct this kind of mistake?". And if we can correct it, then we certainly don't need vision, for rational clarity isn't in need of any vision!

Philolaus: Why vision? Because you may have understood the necessity of Being, but its existence will always remain merely a possibility unless, or until, Being discloses itself. Recall if you will that the Goddess did not say that only order was necessary, but rather both righteousness <u>and</u> order together set him forth on that road.

Glaucon: I could never understand why she included righteousness; is not thought and order sufficient? Anyway, I don't see any particular need to link these two ideas together.

Philolaus: Do you say there is no connection or is it that you haven't noticed any?

Glaucon: What do you mean, haven't noticed?

Philolaus: I think you are waiting for me to convince you. And I think it might be better if I could ask you to reflect on your own experience and then ask you to decide on this matter. Have you observed that whenever we go beyond something we consider fair or right, our thoughts seem to collect around that event, making us reflect upon it whether we want to or not? In some cases are they not like a veritable swarm of thoughts hovering over the event?

Glaucon: Without a doubt, that is true.

Philolaus: And would you not say that they increase, becoming more and more troublesome as the event remembered is thought unjust?

Glaucon: Very true.

Philolaus: And would you also say you have experienced those moments when an event in the past is recalled as a vice or unrighteous only to discover at a later date, for one reason or another, that you were wrong in your judgement and had actually been correct or righteous?

Glaucon: Yes, that has happened.

Philolaus: And after that did you notice that you thought about it less and less?

Glaucon: Yes, but there are other events that I recall or am reminded of by others that I take pleasure in recalling and reflecting upon, and have plenty of thoughts about.

Philolaus: True, and to add to that should we not also consider those events when we are not sure ourselves about our actions being right or not; then we become like members of a jury arguing among themselves about the justice of some matter. Here too thoughts hound us.

Glaucon: Yes, I would certainly agree to that.

Philolaus: And in all these cases are we not adding to ourselves in glorifying ourselves, diminishing ourselves when we condemn ourselves, and mixed when in conflict?

Glaucon: True.

Philolaus: And is not righteousness when we don't go beyond what is fair and just?

Glaucon: Yes.

Philolaus: Are we not then freed from having to reflect upon our past and released from the moods that often accompany those reflections, when we do not exceed what is fair and right?

Glaucon: Yes.

Philolaus: And so, we can be content to remain in ourselves, not needing any increase or decrease. If this is the way of things then we can say it is the order of our universe. Further, would you not say that in being righteous we can participate in a state of mind that permits our deeper involvement in philosophy, since our minds are freed from all those other concerns?

Glaucon: Yes.

Philolaus: So, because of order and righteousness we can become more philosophical, if that is our choice?

Glaucon: Yes, I think I see your point. Anyway I agree that one should act as righteous as possible. However, I recall in that same part of Parmenides' poem there was something I simply could not accept. In fact I have heard you argue that any Gods' divinity could be questioned if ignorance could be charged against them. Now, if you hold that, must you not agree that Being, in so far as it is limited, must also be small and weak when compared with the unlimited? A limited Being, Philolaus, is imperfect.

Philolaus: But if its limitation is on account of order then it would also embody beauty as well as perfection.

Glaucon: I don't see this. Why does order and beauty mean something is limited though perfect?

Philolaus: We have only spoken of this in general, but it is true for all the arts. Take Daidalos, Metion's son or Theodorus the Samian or any of our really good sculptors; do you imagine you could believe that those works of theirs which best embodied the principles of symmetry, balance, proportion, and harmony could be added to or taken away from without diminishing their beauty?

Glaucon: No. I don't think I could believe that.

Philolaus: And possessing the principles of symmetry, balance, proportion and harmony, would you say it lacks the elements of order?

Glaucon: Impossible.

Philolaus: Well then, take another and answer if you will. Could you possibly believe that the hymn of praise of Tynichos of Chalcis, which all the world sings and certainly of all the songs among our people the one most loved, could be changed without affecting its beauty or order?

Glaucon: No, not that either.

Philolaus: Let's try another art. Consider the dramas of Sophocles, Euripides, and those of lofty Aeschylus and contrast them with those of the lesser playwrights; now can you imagine yourself or any man who has not felt restless and cheated when he views a drama whose parts are only loosely connected and even with some parts missing? Do we not reflect upon our experiences, especially those which have been designed for such reflections and so are naturally led to analyze a play, and when we find it lacks unity are we not like a man who has been invited to a banquet only to find that while the evening is still young the host has run out of food and wine? Certainly, in the same way, we are even more sadly disappointed when we discover in the works of some dramatists or sculptors that their vision is lacking and so they can not provide us with a vehicle to gain pleasure in that kind of contemplation which shares not in anything artificial and imperfect but seeks to capture in ideas the nature and dynamics of our reality. For it is when we are able to unite into one all the parts harmoniously that we are able to participate and enjoy the artists' vision.

Glaucon: Yes, I can appreciate that.

Philolaus: Well then you can see that any change, once a work has achieved that mark of beauty, diminishes its beauty and lessens its perfection. And since you have grasped how the idea of perfection is naturally the other side of beauty, you can now see that the idea of Being necessarily includes the idea of perfection; since it too needs nothing and nothing can be added to or taken away from the nature of Being.

Glaucon: Well we got here but I'm not sure I feel as secure with the idea of Being being perfect as I can with beauty. However, I don't really understand how this idea of perfection in beauty has any importance in the pursuit of philosophy; and that's not because I don't appreciate the beauty in the youths I find around here and elsewhere.

Philolaus: Try for a moment to follow my reasoning, but not as an exercise in logic, rather see if you can play seriously with this idea because, you see, you have already seen all the parts necessary to make this clear... and all you need do is reflect along with me as we go together.

Glaucon: Go ahead, I'll follow.

Philolaus: In the experience of beauty are we not led to wonder? Are we not held fast to the moment, are we not roused from within ourselves, does it not awaken us to an astonishment and without effort of any kind bring us to the realization that what has been revealed to us gives us confidence that inherent to what is there is something more noble and with an integrity that we have forgotten, yet once seen we bring it to our own interior and contemplate it? Further, would you not agree that this is wholly impossible were it not that the very idea of perfection permeates and is inseparable from all our experiences of beauty, yet throughout all this it is not a physical thing we experience but wholly idea, an idea that leads us to the recognition that that which is, Being, is in the midst of each and offers us a glimpse of reality or Being. Thus, these appearances, as it were, bring us not illusion, because in their very appearance they "rightfully appear to be," revealing themselves to be full of beauty and intelligence.

Glaucon: You know there are times when I don't know what to do with what you say, either your questions or answers. I would like to agree with you, maybe because that's the way I would like it to be too, however, I can see one thing at least and that is that it seems to me that this is not a matter of logically following, but rather an entering into and seeing. You see I'm used to dealing with ideas and if they seem to me to be logical I usually go along with them, but this seems different.

Philolaus: See it dimly now and later it will become clearer as you reflect upon it. Further, let me add another part, for I am sure you will find an opportunity to reflect upon this later. Beauty is a sign of the presence of order and intelligence and whether you proceed either by beauty or intelligence you can discover the same thing.

Glaucon: And that is?

Philolaus: That we do not confront either a hostile or indifferent world. And what we are the cosmos shares. What we call the appearances, what is apprehended through the senses and about which we fashion opinions, can be understood, and so there is a righteousness of the appearances, for mind must penetrate everywhere. This activity is what is called, by some, "saving the appearances."

Glaucon: I will have to consider this; it might be possible, but it seems to me that on the one hand Philolaus, you find thoughts are like the furies, returning to haunt us for our misdeeds, and then on the other you have thought and Being at the heart of reality. But if thoughts are like the furies then what you regard as reality is more like the shades or ghosts of Hades wandering about this way and that; surely such a view makes life and death a horror and more mad than rational.

Philolaus: I understand how you came to that, but consider, how many words do you know that can be included in the idea of thought?

Glaucon: What?

Philolaus: Well, take any idea, or an image, a probable account, or even a belief; are these called thoughts, each and every one of them?

Glaucon: Yes.

Philolaus: Would you not add to that list such terms as understanding, insight and all kinds of reflection?

Glaucon: Yes, but then how do you choose among them and in what sense does Parmenides mean thought? For I do see what you mean and I hardly think Parmenides would be saying that belief and Being were one and the same.

Philolaus: Good. Then consider, would you not expect Parmenides to reflect that same tradition he frequently alludes to in the Journey? There are many references from Homer's works which I am sure you noticed, and so are we not obliged to follow his lead and ask how that term, thought, is used in Homer?

Glaucon: I think that's a good way to proceed.

Philolaus: Do you recall from Homer when that most excellent of singers, whom the Muse loved, was in the house of wise Alkinoos of the Phaiakians, and he sang the story of how Apollo had prophesied to

Agamemnon in sacred Pytho and told him that the designs of Zeus against the Trojans and Danaans would only begin when the best of the Achaians were quarreling among themselves?

Glaucon: Yes.

Philolaus: Have you reflected that after the singer described the quarrel between Odysseus and Achilles he said Agamemnon felt joy in his thought (nous)?

Glaucon: What do you find interesting in that?

Philolaus: Well, since Agamemnon was told the prophecy and had reflected upon it he was able to grasp the meaning of what he saw. In that very moment he saw the fulfillment of the prophecy and, at the same time, recognized that he was directly watching the first step in the design of mighty Zeus; he knew, too, that this was the beginning of the misfortune that would descend upon the hated Trojans. This kind of seeing is with the mind alone and is an unclouded vision that can penetrate into not merely the human dimension but also into the divine significance of what is seen. Seeing with the mind, in this way, is to exercise what Homer calls "nous." Now is this way of seeing captured in the word thought, or thinking?

Glaucon: I would certainly say no.

Philolaus: Then we agree that we should consider this way of using the mind not the same as merely thinking thoughts?

Glaucon: Certainly.

Philolaus: Then when Parmenides says that to think and to be are the same, or that we will not find thinking without Being, we should recall he means "nous" and hesitate before considering this to mean that Being is merely a thought.

Glaucon: I follow your meaning, but is "nous," or thought, something that only belongs to man or is it something divine that man shares with the gods? For if only man possesses it I would say one thing, but if shared with the gods, another.

Philolaus: I recall it said in Homer's <u>Iliad</u>: "But always the mind of Zeus is a stronger thing than a man's mind.", and the word mind is, of course, the same word "nous." Thus, would you agree "nous" is of the divine, shared with the divine, and becomes the bridge to the divine.

Glaucon: I see what you mean.

Philolaus: Does that mean you agree?

Glaucon: Well the most I can say is that I can't find any way to reject what you are saying, but my mind still returns to the idea that if the Universe were infinite, whether there is order or not, it would still not be limited, for surely, nothing could contain the infinite.

Philolaus: And what if it is contained?

Glaucon: Then it would be finite, yet immense.

Philolaus: Does not thought embrace all?

Glaucon: In what way?

Philolaus: Mind encompasses what is, embraces what is and so it is that which encompasses and, since there is nothing apart from it, it contains and limits what is. Yet, Glaucon, neither of the terms, finite or infinite, can define Being. For both what is encompassed and what encompasses simply is.

Glaucon: Perhaps it is as you say but I would like to return to something you mentioned before and I never fully understood. This idea of a probable account; why did the Goddess tell Parmenides only a probable account? If it's really a vision of Truth, why teach him the probable arrangement of the universe when the Goddess could, I suppose, reveal truths? And if you think belief is insufficient, why teach it? If there is a difference between accepting a belief or accepting a probable account, I don't see it.

Philolaus: Are not all accounts of the Universe probable?

Glaucon: I'm not sure, in what way do you mean?

Philolaus: You might consider it in this way: words and ideas are like the colors and images the artist or craftsman uses in fashioning his works. The portraits or pictures done by an artist are like our views of the Universe. And while each artist tries to capture as truly as he can the particular distinguishing mark of his subject, would you say any artist to your knowledge has ever achieved perfection, or would you say there might be someone who could not tell the difference between the object and its copy?

Glaucon: No. It is unlikely that someone would mistake a painting for the real.

Philolaus: And would you not also say that no one can find the true and perfect portrait of anyone, if we mean by true, a perfect likeness.

Glaucon: Yes, I would say that too.

Philolaus: And are not accounts of the universe pictures made of words and shaped into images and some are better executed or fashioned than others, but would you not agree that none can be called true. For if that were so then the two would be indistinguishable from each other.

Glaucon: Yes, then the true would perfectly mirror the other and so be an exact copy.

Philolaus: Then as each account is similar to the works of art and can not be regarded as true, so too for those pictures of the Universe that we fashion with words and ideas, for they too are probable though some are more probable than others. And since they are not to be regarded as true, should we not call them by some other name, say, opinion?

Glaucon: You might call it opinion but there is more to art than copying faithfully some object.

Philolaus: Yes, there is more to art than merely copying. But in either case when we judge we do so by the presence of those qualities which render all things intelligible. However, the difference between art and nature lies in the maker. For when those qualities are present in things we assign a divine maker as the source, but when these same qualities are present in a work of a man we call him an artist. So you see, art does not copy nature, but the principles of things and their generation.

Glaucon: Let me ask you this: If as you say art is to the principles of things and their generation, then what, in the same way, is to Being and its generation?

Philolaus: The true cannot be copied; it has neither shape nor form, but if you consider it carefully, perhaps you can say simply: Is. However, if you do you should be careful not to confuse it with anything you might call existing.

Glaucon: But doesn't Parmenides say that Being has the shape of a well-rounded sphere? And if that is so wouldn't you agree that if Being is within the limits of that sphere then what is outside the sphere must be non-Being?

Philolaus: But would you not say that a man is foolish if he looks above our city for sails unfurling in the air simply because someone said that a city is like a ship at sea?

Glaucon: Certainly I would.

Philolaus: Well then, Parmenides said Being was <u>like</u> a sphere, not that Being was a sphere. Consider the use of the simile and you will see the point Parmenides was making was to dramatically show that Being is not lacking anywhere; in other words it reaches out equally and so it is equal on all sides. Further, he adds, does he not, that there is no non-Being which could mark its boundary. Would you not agree then, that this is indeed a simile and not to be taken literally. Actually, Glaucon, this is, as you know, the same problem as with Parmenides' use of the word *signs,* because it would be a failing not to see that a sign of something is different from the thing, just as the signs of war are different from war itself.

Glaucon: Oh yes, I recall your saying that otherwise we would conclude that there are more tales of the road than that it simply: Is.

Philolaus: Then you agree when we say this account is not Truth itself but only approaches it?

Glaucon: Would it be fair to call that a probable account?

Philolaus: Yes.

Glaucon: Yes?

Philolaus: And is it believable?

Glaucon: I believe it could be probable!

Philolaus: Well, I see you are becoming more cautious with your words. Is it likely that you believe it is probable because you haven't seen the grounds or argument that would demonstrate it and so not-knowing but wishing it might be true, you believe?

Glaucon: Yes, however try as I might, Philolaus, I still don't find these ideas of Parmenides, or your own way of looking at them as convincing as I would like.

Philolaus: That's likely because trying to convince someone, even ourselves, is not what we do here.

Glaucon: Now I know I don't understand; I thought that's what philosophy was all about.

Philolaus: There are some who try to convince others or to inculcate some belief but we are not interested in certainty or belief when understanding is possible. Let's look at it again. Suppose a man were to ask you the best route to follow from Elea to Athens and you discovered it was very important to him to arrive there safely but that he had little or no experience traveling, which of you would more than likely feel the need to be certain about the truth of the advise, you or he?

Glaucon: I imagine he would want to be convinced about the right route.

Philolaus: And would you need to convince yourself about the proper route from Elea to Athens, if you have travelled it many times before and have, indeed, just come from that journey yesterday?

Glaucon: But, Philolaus, the example shows the need to be convinced before a philosophical journey, so you should be convincing me as I should the traveler. But you say you don't... I don't understand.

Philolaus: Our approach is not to convince by argument but to share our way of understanding, which requires a mode of seeing and that seeing is itself to travel along the road of the Goddess. And by returning to Parmenidean thought and reflecting upon it, expressing it in our own words, and before others, we see ourselves grow and develop in that way in which a man is most benefitted.

Glaucon: Yes, this may very well be true, yet when I reflect upon Parmenidean thought I often hear not one voice, but two.

Philolaus: And whose voices do you hear?

Glaucon: Yours and Parmenides'.

Philolaus: And do we say the same things or different things about these matters?

Glaucon: I think you have represented his thought fairly but one thing stands out in sharp contrast from all the rest of what you have said, and it is this very thing that puzzles me, so I would like to hear what you have to say about it.

Philolaus: What is it that troubles you?

Glaucon: Well, on the one hand Parmenides thinks all this is Being, and I think I have grasped that better than I previously had, but you call it the One; isn't Being different from the One?

Philolaus: I would like to explore this question with you but you may not be able to follow me in the way I would wish, although it would not be because we lack good will. I should be glad if I could explain it to you, but your question requires we abandon all images in our search for meaning, and further, we must call upon all our experience in discussion, for that alone will make it possible for us to distinguish between the One itself and the One that is; but without this ability and effort we shall fail utterly in our attempt.

Glaucon: I'd rather not go through all that at this time, why not turn it around and let me judge your answer to this question, then I'll see if I want to go into what seems to me to be a huge task.

Philolaus: That is fair. Well, Being itself is what is, and since there is no other it can be called One; since that One itself banishes both any otherness and is also nameless it cannot, strictly speaking, be called either Being or the One. However, in another way, since Being is what is and what is is One, it can be referred to as One. Again, consider the matter in this way: if all the terms Parmenides uses in his account of Being are reducible to Being and, since Being itself admits of no plurality, this Being is One.

Glaucon: I'd say you won that one and if you don't object I'll postpone hearing that discussion for some other time. What shall we call it, One or Being?

Philolaus: Or should we call it, "Being, The One?"

Glaucon: Call it "Being, The One," that will certainly give me something to think about.

Philolaus: And what of you, Erotima? It looks like you have a question to raise.

Erotima: Yes, Philolaus, I do have a question that has been puzzling me. You see, I have often thought that questions were merely another of man's weapons with which he battles his fellowman, but clearly both you and Parmenides regard them differently. For if Being can be described in terms like clinging and embracing, it must be that you find in love the image you need to describe reality. But do you really find a similar kinship between questions and love?

Philolaus: Recall, if you will, that Being can be said to be all embracing not because it has arms and such but because its beauty is so full and penetrating that it can be said to be embracing itself. However, it would be well to remember that it is in respect to Being that all names have been spoken, hence while these terms can be used in respect to Being, it is beyond names.

Erotima: I think I will have to give that more thought, but what of questions and love?

Philolaus: There is a natural affinity and bond between love and questions and I expect you already know that since your name, Erotima, means and echoes love and questions.

Erotima: Yes, that is true, but I would still like to know what you think of it.

Philolaus: Well then, consider the way lovers are together; the way they are drawn together; they awaken from a deep slumber of forgetfulness as they draw, from themselves, their best to share with one another; their presence together is itself a vow of their willingness to mold a present and future in which knowing and loving are embraced, so too a question awakens oneself, alerts us to the moment, brings from within us an answer for our consideration and reflection and, in addition, it returns us once more to the realization that while meaningful change, growth and development are intrinsic to man, it is most clearly perceived when these two, love and reason, become one.

Scene 6:

Erotima concludes. The setting returns to scene 1.

Erotima: This, then, is the story, as I have been able to reconstruct it. And in reflecting on it now I am reminded that when I first began giving this account I found I was acting as if I was still a priestess and expected my account of this vision would be unquestioned; I believed objections and criticisms were more directed at me than my message. But somehow I knew my experience with Parmenidean thought was more central to my being and so I learned to avoid what certainly would have led to my own blindness. I was able to do this only by remembering those things the communion with which causes one to see again the source of oneself.

My previous concerns with the thought from Persia, Zoroastrianism, have been resolved, however, I think time will show that the dynamics of that belief will eventually gain a victory, and so sweep over us. It is the opinion of those at Delphi and Dodona that this belief has a demonic life of its own, for when you think you have destroyed it you find it returns in a slightly different form, each time to do battle again. When it is victorious it brings with it a dark age that increases man's sufferings and when it is defeated men awaken to a new sense of freedom and creativity. We feel that it takes no prophet to see that this conflict will continue until the very nature of belief is discovered and its form clearly apprehended.

For myself I found my familiarity with the beliefs of Zoroastrians helped me understand what Parmenides was saying. I could see clearly that while he may have been addressing himself to others besides the Zoroastrians, such as Heraclitus and his followers, those others had to be in some respect similar to the Zoroastrians.

So too my experience and studies of Homer and all the other good poets helped my understanding so that now I have come to realize why the numerous expressions from Homer, Hesiod, and other divine poets are included in Parmenides' poem. Truths revealed to man, from whatever source, are divine and can be compared with each other, and so Parmenides is in the company of men like Homer and Hesiod. He bridged what was thought impossible; he made the journey from utter darkness to the light and found in each, pure Being.

Selected Bibliography

The works cited below have either directly or indirectly influenced my thought and should not, of course, be considered as a complete bibliography of the literature on Parmenides. A recent bibliography on the literature, in English, can be found in "Pre-Socratic Studies, 1953-1966," *Classical World,* 60 (1966-67), 15759, by E. L. Minar. In respect to Homer, both *The Iliad* and *The Odyssey,* as well as Plato's works, I have had reference to the Loeb Classical Library. In addition I have had reference to the Rouse translation of *The Great Dialogues of Plato.*

Bicknell, P. J., "Parmenides' Refutation of Motion and an Implication," *Phronesis,* 12 (1967), 1-5.

Bowra, C. M., "The Proem of Parmenides," *Classical Philology,* 32 (1937), 97-112.

Brumbaugh, R. S., *Plato On The One,* Port Washington, New York, Kennikat Press, 1973.

Cornford, F. M., *From Religion to Philosophy,* London, Edward Arnold, 1912.

Plato's Theory of Knowledge, London, Routledge & Kegan Paul, 1934.

Cornford, F. M., "A New Fragment of Parmenides," *Classical Review,* 49 (1935), 122-23.

Cornford, F. M., *Plato's Cosmology,* London, Routledge Kegan Paul, 1937.

Cornford, F. M., *Plato and Parmenides,* London, Routledge Kegan Paul, 1939.

Darmesteter, James, *The Sacred Books of the East,* vol. iv, Oxford, The Clarendon Press, 1895.

Dolin, E. F., Jr., "Parmenides and Hesiod," *Harvard Studies in Classical Philology,* 66. (1962), 93-98.

Duchesne-Guillemin, J., *Zoroastrianism, Symbols and Values,* New York, Harper Torchbooks, 1970.

Eliade, Mircea, *Shamanism: Archaic Technique of Ecstasy,* tr. W. R. Trask, New York, Bollingen Foundation, 1964.

Fowler, H. N., *Plato:* vols. I, III, IV, V, VI, (Loeb Classical Library), Cambridge, Mass., Harvard University Press, 1970.

Furley, David, "Parmenides of Elea," s.v. in *The Encyclopedia of Philosophy,* New York, Macmillan and Free Press, 1967.

Furth, Montgomery, "Elements of Eleatic Ontology," *Journal of the History of Philosophy,* 7 (1968), 111-32.

Havelock, Eric A., "Parmenides and Odysseus," *Harvard Studies in Classical Philology,* 63, (1958), 133-43.

Jaeger, Werner, *The Theology of the Early Greek Philosophers,* Oxford, Clarendon Press, 1947.

Jameson, G., "'Well-Rounded Truth' and Circular Thought in Parmenides," *Phronesis,* 3 (1958), 15-30.

Jonas, Hans, *The Gnostic Religion,* Boston, Beacon Press, 1963.

Kahn, Charles, "The Greek Verb 'To Be' and the Concept of Being," *Foundations of Language,* 2 (1966), 245-65.

Kirk, G. S., *Heraclitus: The Cosmic Fragments,* Cambridge, Cambridge University Press, 1954.

Kirk, G. S.,*The Songs of Homer,* Cambridge, Cambridge University Press, 1962.

Kirk, G. S.,and Michael C. Stokes, "Parmenides' Refutation of Motion," *Phronesis,* 5 (1960), 1-4.

Knight, Thomas S., "Parmenides and the Void," *Philology and Phenomenological Research,* 19, (1958-59), 524-31.

Lee, Edward N., "On the Metaphysics of the Image in Plato's *Timaeus,*" *The Monist,* 50, (1966), 341-68.

Lloyd, G. E. R., *Polarity and Analogy: Two Types of Argumentation in Early Greek Thought,* Cambridge, Cambridge University Press, 1966.

Loenen, J. H. M. M., *Parmenides, Melissus, Gorgias: A Reinterpretation of Eleatic Philosophy,* Assen, Van Gorcum, 1959.

Long, A. A., "The Principles of Parmenides' Cosmogony," *Phronesis,* 8 (1963), 90-108.

Masani, R., *Zoroastrianism,* New York, Macmillan Company, 1968.

Merlan, P., *From Platonism to Neoplatonism,* The Hague, Martinus Nijhoff, 1960.

Meuli, K., "Scythica," *Hermes,* 70 (1935), 121-76.

Mills, L. H., *The Sacred Books of the East,* vol. xxxi, Oxford, The Clarendon Press, 1887.

Moulton, J. H., *Early Zoroastrianism,* London, Allen & Unwin, 1913.

Mourelatos, Alexander P. D., "Heraclitus Fr.114," *American Journal of Philology,* 86 (1965), 258-66.

Mourelatos, Alexander P. D.,"The Real, Appearances, and Human Error in Early Greek Philosophy," *The Review of Metaphysics,* 19 (1965), 346-65.

Mourelatos, Alexander P. D.,*The Route of Parmenides,* New Haven and London, Yale University Press, 1970.

O'Brien, Elmer, *The Essential Plotinus,* New York, Mentor Press, 1964.

Owen, G. E. L., "Plato and Parmenides on the Timeless Present," *The Monist,* 50 (1966), 317-40.

Rouse, W. H. D., *The Great Dialogues of Plato,* New York, The New American Library, 1956.

Seligman, Paul, *The "Apeiron" of Anaximander: A Study in the Origin and Function of Metaphysical Ideas,* London, Athlone Press, 1962.

Siegel, Rodulph, "Parmenides and the Void: Some Comments on the Paper of

Thomas S. Knight," *Philosophy and Phenomenological Research,* 22 (1961-62), 264-66.

Solmsen, Friedrich, *Hesiod and Aeschylus,* Cornell Studies in Classical Philology, 30, Ithaca, Cornell University Press, 1949.

Stanford, William Bedell, *Greek Metaphor: Studies in Theory and Practice,* Oxford, B. Blackwell, 1936.

Stanford, William Bedell, *The Ulysses Theme: A Study in the Adaptability of a Traditional Hero,* Oxford, B. Blackwell, 1954.

Taran, L., *Parmenides,* Princeton University, 1965.

Tugwell, Simon, "The Way of Truth," *Classical Quarterly,* N.S. 14 (1964), 36-41.

Verdenius, W. J., "Parmenides' Conception of Light," *Mnemosyne,* 2 (1949), 116-31.

Vlastos, Gregory, "Equality and Justice in Early Greek Cosmologies," *Classical Philology,* 42 (1947), 156-78.

Vlastos, Gregory, "On Heraclitus," *American Journal of Philology,* 76 (1955), 337-63.

West, M. L., *Hesiod: Theogony: Edited with Prolegomena and Commentary,* Oxford, Clarendon Press, 1966.

Wheelwright, P., *The Presocratics,* New York, The Odyssey Press, 1966.

Plato's Parmenides as the Paradigm for Metaphysics and Theology

Pierre: Good morning it is to you, Joseph. Join me here for coffee. Say, what are those pictures sticking out of your book? They look interesting; they just might relate to that book you have there, and it seems like it is one of Plato's dialogues. From the looks of it I might guess it is one of the many good translations by the Balboas.

Joseph: Thanks, I'll join you for a cup. Yes, you are right, and it is Plato's *Parmenides*. I can't say that I get much out of it, but I am trying. One day I am in it and the next day I am ready to throw it away. It may yet become somewhat like the difficulties I had with my study of the *Republic*. I had found it very puzzling until I found a way into it. As for the pictures, they are of the goddess Athena. I find it curious that she could become an object of worship. I say that because their religion and some of their philosophy is still a bit remote from me. I admire the way artists portrayed Athena, but I have no idea of why or how she became an object of devotion to the Ancient Greeks. Anyway it is not easy to understand religions, Ancient Greek, or any of them.

Pierre: You caught two fish on the same line. Which of the two are you going to talk about first?

Joseph: Well, I have nothing but puzzles about both. I would like to begin with a puzzle about Plato's *Parmenides*, since as you know, it is a recollection of Cephalos' recollection of Antiphon's recollection of Pythodorus' recollection of a dialogue that took place when Zeno and Parmenides came to Athens to celebrate the Great Panathenaea. Is it fair to ask why Plato repeats the theme of recollection so many times? Now, it may seem strange, but I would also like to know why a festival to Athena is mentioned in the dialogue. Do you see any meaning in these things? Or is it merely cosmetic, so my question may be frivolous?

Pierre: No, actually your questions turn on a curious issue: How do you know when a given answer truly answers a question? Say Joseph, what is it about Athena and that dialogue of Plato's that caught your attention?

Joseph: I like the idea of Athena as the personification of wisdom, but is there more to it than this? Can't an intro simply be a polite way of saying hello or setting the scene for a drama to play out?

Pierre: You have, of course, heard that many of Plato's dialogues have introductions and that they anticipate the entire dialogue, but is it also possible that one dialogue can be seen as the completion of another? Indeed, is it possible that some dialogues are like philosophical triads that link together and complete three dialogues? Some, you know, might even be arranged in sets of four.

Joseph: I would like to see that. Which three?

Pierre: Plato's *Ion*, his *Republic*, and the *Parmenides*.

Joseph: That's good for me; I've gone over all three.

Pierre: Then consider the introduction to these three dialogues. We could ask why the Goddess Athena is mentioned in the *Parmenides*, why Bendis, the Moon goddess, who is akin to Artemis, is in the *Republic*, and why Asclepios is in Plato's *Ion*.

Joseph: No, I can't say I have linked any three together. Do you think Plato's reference to these religious festivals is doing that? Apart from that, do you say this possible linkage has any meaning?

Pierre: Since you have read these dialogues let me ask you a couple of questions. Since the idea of art is explored in the *Ion* and Socrates shows Ion that he does not possess an art, are we not left wondering if Socrates possesses an art? And is it possible that he fits all the conditions for possessing the art of divination?

Joseph: I recall discussions that raised that very point.

Pierre: Doesn't Plato's *Republic* expand the idea of art? Plato outlines a course of study, an arduous practice, and difficult training that is crowned with the art of dialectic. Does he not advance the idea of art even further since he adds that it is through this art that one truly benefits the soul? Does he not say that the culmination of the study is akin to what Homer calls becoming in the image and likeness of God?

Joseph: Yes, indeed, and when I first heard of it I found that claim astonishing. And, sure enough, he does make clear that only the application of a knowledge that benefits the subject should be called an art.

Pierre: However, would you not agree that the dialectic described in his Book Six and Seven of the *Republic* is only an outline and, so, lacks precision and depth?

Joseph: Yes, I always wondered about that. After he takes the time to outline so much, he spends only a few sentences on the dialectic.

Pierre: Yes, the dialectic is packed into less than two paragraphs in the *Republic*. However, it is in the *Parmenides* that he unfolds the dialectic of what is called the One-Many problem. It is a model for the exploration and contemplation of the essential ideas of Platonic metaphysics.

The development of the unity of these triadic dialogues has dramatic features, analogical structures, and mythological elements that weave together a tapestry of philosophical ideas that present a spiritual vision for mankind. Thus, we can take Plato's *Republic* as the mean between the extremes, and we can contrast these dialogues to see their similar and dissimilar themes.

Joseph: So you think that the *Parmenides* completes the dialectic of Plato's *Republic*, so the *Republic* completes the idea of art and the philosopher in the *Ion*. Now, that is interesting. What else?

Pierre: Well, we can compare the theological or mythological themes and note that each cites its own uniqueness in the introduction of the dialogue.

Joseph: How do you see the mythological theme playing out in the triad? Are these references to the gods and goddesses really playing some symbolic role? Are they of any philosophical significance?

Pierre: Consider the introductions to these dialogues: In Plato's *Ion*, Socrates engages Ion, who has just won first price for reciting Homer at the feast of Asclepios, the God of the art of medicine, and cures him of his belief that the reciter-interpreter possesses an art.

In the *Republic*, Socrates went down to the Piraeus with Glaucon to witness the new Thracian night festival of Bendis, the Moon Goddess, the goddess of the hunt and medicine, and purged those in the house of Cephalos of their false beliefs about justice. In pursuing the nature of art he leads those about him to the highest kind of benefit, wisdom. The practice and learning to reach this goal became the art of the philosopher king. As you know, the culmination of this learning is the dialectic, which brings one to the experience of the most brilliant light of Being, the Idea of the Good, which leads to the Good, or the One. However, the description that Plato gives of the Good, or the One, and the Idea of the Good, or the Brilliant light of Being, are presented analogically and allegorically and so lack a certain precision, but not scope.

In Plato's *Parmenides* Zeno and Parmenides went to Athens to witness the Great Panathenaea, celebrating the birth of Athena. At this time Parmenides is persuaded to give a demonstration of the dialectic. After he rejects the false ideas of how ideas participate, he is urged to give an account of the dialectic. In his example of the dialectic he chooses to explore the One itself, whether the One exists or whether the One does not exist. He goes on to explore this hypothesis by considering the condition of its existence and its nonexistence. In doing so he discusses the four affirmative ways of exploring the One-Many, and the four corresponding ways of rejecting them. This is the model for the exploration of any idea. It provides the model of the dialectic; and with the addition of the One itself, it becomes the means through which the goals of the philosopher king are finally realized.

Joseph: Thanks. I will look forward to exploring these interrelations. You see the triad as the way to the Good. But for all that I still do not see that the One-Many problem has any religious or spiritual significance. Sure it has two sets of four, one positive, one negative, with the One on top of it all. It is supposed to be intellectual fun, yes, but it has nothing to do with anything spiritual, does it? Frankly, if these gods are not objects of what I would call devotion, then I don't really know what good they are. I don't think I am different from other people. How might these people see something spiritual in a religion that I can't find anything spiritual in?

Pierre: Well, Joseph, I always have admired your questions and your spirit. You keep going on even though you face answers to your questions that usually stop others. You have raised something important, and I am not at all sure that any answer, or argument, of mine will satisfy you. Before I try to deal with that theological problem, I wonder if you might share with me what you have found troublesome about the *Parmenides.*

Joseph: I know full well that Athena symbolizes wisdom; but for all that, I fail to understand why Plato opens up the dialogue with a review of a flawed argument about the Many. Zeno had composed it many years earlier and presents a reading of it before Socrates' group of friends. The argument just doesn't make any sense. So why present a bad argument at a festival to celebrate wisdom when it is empty of meaning? Maybe I am asking about something that is foolish to ask. To put it simply, if Parmenides, who Socrates thinks so highly of, let's his close friend and fellow philosopher, Zeno, give a reading of an argument that is at best foolish and at worst empty of all meaning then is he saying that fools start what the wise finish? Shall this be in celebration of Athena? However, for all that, I wonder if I am foolish trying to get answers out of a book that can only be answered by the author. And Plato isn't around to answer them.

Pierre: Would you explain what you understand Zeno's position to be?

Joseph: I'm not sure about explaining it, but I have the Fowler translation[1] here on this piece of paper. I'm using it to compare with the Balboa translation. Here, I'll read it:

> "Zeno, what do you mean by this? That if existences are many, they must be both like and unlike, which is impossible; for the unlike cannot be like, nor the like to be unlike? Is that not your meaning?"

After Socrates gets an agreement from Zeno he comes back saying this:

> "Then if it is impossible for the unlike to be like and the like unlike, it is impossible for existences to be many; for if they were to be many, they would experience the impossible."

Pierre: Thanks for the reading, so now tell me what it is about his argument that leads you to conclude that it is empty of all meaning?

Joseph: At times it just doesn't even make enough sense to explain the problem that I have with it, and at other times I get an answer that seems to make sense—only later to find it doesn't. I get into the question for a while; but after getting nowhere I dump it; and then I find I get back into it, and bang, I repeat this cycle again and again. It seems incomplete to me; like it stands alone for itself, and for me it just doesn't work. I can't find an example that has anything in common with that kind of reasoning. I look at it and say, "Of course things that are like must have features that are unlike, for if they didn't they would be the same." Like you and I: We share some features and so are like, and there are some features about us that are unlike, and if there weren't we would be twins, the same, right? So why does he say that the idea is impossible because unlike can't be like? So what? Well, it leaves me indifferent to it. Yet, how can I reject what others agree with? Then I see it the other way and say to myself, "Of course the same things that are like can't be unlike," and that spins me around again. I end up saying, "It is true and it ain't true." However, I'm still in it without being able to know why I am still in it. I have tried to puzzle my way through it without going anywhere. Maybe it is just that some friends of mine are in it, so I hang around with them. I end up wondering if it can have some meaning. Like, is it supposed to have some spiritual or philosophical meaning that means something and is worth all the effort? Or is Zeno's argument a zero?

Pierre: Actually, it is an interesting argument that he begins with. If we fail to grasp the point of what he is doing, it is likely to diminish our interest in the dialogue. But in your case it sounds like you are busting your head over this dialogue and can't find a way to break through. So, Joseph, why not fill me in on what else you have done to understand Zeno's argument?

Joseph: Usual stuff: I checked out some other translations and none agrees with the other, but no matter which one you chose, it is the same confusion in them all. How can his argument be understood if even translators are uncertain just what his argument is about? I've checked them out, and they differ so widely that if you do understand one of them you can't apply it to the others. Either the argument is so obscure that even translators can't make it clear, or one is good and the others not, and I can't figure out if any of them are any better than the others. Sure they are similar yet their differences exclude the others. Consider these four statements and you tell me if you have found any one better than the other. What difference does it make even if one is better?

The first translates it as "if Things are many"; the second, "if Beings are many"; the third, "if Existences are many"; and the fourth, "if Realities are many." How can you proceed to discuss this issue when the experts can't agree? Do you pick the one that seems to you best? Is it all relative? Is this a Greek language problem?

Pierre: No, but it raises an interesting issue. All of those translations are possible; each raises its own issues. These four ideas—Things, Existences, Beings and Realities—can be substituted for the one Greek word, *onta*. Each can be substituted for that one word, so they all qualify as translations. So these four ideas are the many that can be substituted for the one term. They all differ from one another nonetheless: they can be compared and contrasted. That means, does it not, that they are alike and unlike. Now, what do you think: is it possible or impossible for each to communicate the same thing?

Joseph: I doubt if we can say which one is better than the other. Just what was Zeno, or Plato, doing? Or just what are the translators doing for that matter. Are we dumb or is Plato? I can't see my way, nor can I possibly communicate what I don't understand myself. For me it has nothing good in it, it's not just empty, it's not even mixed with anything good. Or are Plato and Socrates doing something obvious in that dialogue that we overlook?

Pierre: Joseph, let me offer something. These four ideas are not all the same; rather each is different from the others. In addition, they may be arranged in groups, or subclasses, and if you examine them in this way you might find something interesting.

Joseph: I'm for it.

Pierre: Good. Then of the four would you pick out the one that best expresses the problem of the One and the Many? Which of the four would you say is central to Parmenides? Is he interested in natural philosophy and so would choose to discuss "Things" and "Existences" or "Beings" and "Realities"?

Joseph: Now, that was helpful, it took me out of my do-nothing state. I'd say that the idea of things can simply be the stuff of the world around me; and since this stuff exists I'd say both things and existences fit the everyday world; and I'd add that it is not likely to be what Parmenides is interested in since he says what Is is One. He also says that only Being Is.

Pierre: True, and the terms Things and Existences describe appearances, do they not? For if there are things, they surely must have some kind of existence, must they not?

Joseph: Sure thing.

Pierre: And what of Beings and Realities?

Joseph: Beings and Realities are another pair. However, Beings and Realities are likely to be more of what Parmenides would be interested in, and they are what he would call Reality, right?

Pierre: Correct you are there. Would you agree that each of these pairs that we have called appearance and reality have a sameness to them, don't' they?

Joseph: Again, sure thing.

Pierre: And these pairs could not be more dissimilar could they? For their differences make them dissimilar. For appearance and reality are essentially different, are they not?

Joseph: Right.

Pierre: So, these pairs of like and unlike are essentially different?

Joseph: Sure thing.

Pierre: And, if they are so different, could the ones that you just called like be those you called unlike? For how could reality be like appearance, or appearance like reality?

Joseph: Why no, I don't think that could be.

Pierre: Or could those you call unlike be like those others?

Joseph: No, that would be impossible—at least if I keep in mind what I just said about them being in totally different pairs.

Pierre: Could you make the one pair be like the other without making them undergo something impossible? Or could the unlike pair become like, and the like pair become unlike, without either pair going through impossibilities?

Joseph: I like what you are doing.

Pierre: Then if these different ways of describing these pairs was helpful, we can now ask another kind of question.

Joseph: But wait a minute! Zeno wasn't taking these terms in pairs. He just used one Greek word, right? Parmenides is using complex ideas that are theories rather than single ideas, isn't he?

Pierre: True, I was just reviewing the terms and contrasting them since each is possible, and Socrates will expose each of them for analysis later in the dialogue.

Joseph: That's true. I do recall he does that. I even liked it when Socrates says he would be amazed if Zeno could show him that the One is many and the many one. Maybe I wanted to make sure I grasped everything from the very beginning rather than skip a puzzle and just walk my way through it. It may not be the right way to go, but I seem stuck on this way, somewhat like a kid who can't let go of anything and tries to keep everything for himself, at least that's what I've been told I was like.

Pierre: Likely, but you can challenge what you have learned in the past since you know it is no longer helping you in your present.

Joseph: Then I would rather like to talk about realities being many because the idea of Being is more abstract for me. However, if we were not sure about what he means by "realities are many" we would be in a fix.

Pierre: Then let's reflect for a moment. Is the position "realities are many" different from "realities are one"? Because if they were one that would mean, would it not, that the realities taken together are one and not many?

Joseph: Sure.

Pierre: So if he says realities are many, then each of them must be different while still having enough sameness with the others to be able to say that each is a reality.

Joseph: Seems true.

Pierre: However, each of the many must be a one, or they couldn't possibly be many, and to say that realities are many is merely to stress the obvious since the idea of realities is plural. To say that it is many, doesn't add anything to it, does it?

Joseph: I totally agree with that. I don't see that anyone can get anywhere with it, yet it is the reasons he gives for rejecting it that bug me. I can agree with his conclusion but not with the reasons he cites. So his reasoning just leaves me as unaffected and unresponsive as I am to evangelical door knockers. I sit back and say "So why can't like things be unlike?"

Pierre: Well, we do know that many translators use the terms you just described for the one Greek word, don't we? For the same word had the same set of possible meanings even in the Greek.

Joseph: Yes, that's true enough, curious as it is. You have an interesting way to explore Zeno's argument. It seems to spin around the words like and unlike. Now I wonder about the use of like and unlike, but let's put that aside. You got me to pick out the pairs to make your point, and I don't know if that way of reasoning would work if they weren't pairs, or sets, with two members. The idea of likeness and unlikeness looms large, you know what I mean?

Pierre: Yes, I do. All creation presupposes the possibility of likeness; otherwise, how could there be model and copy?

Joseph: I like that, but if you don't mind I just got an idea. Maybe, just maybe, the different realities do not form or belong to classes and subclasses. If so we might escape the conclusion we reached.

Pierre: Well, their differences must be such that they don't fall into any set of classes or subclasses. Then, how different must they be from each other yet each still to be a reality?

Joseph: Well, OK, they would still have to fall into the class of reality. I see that.

Pierre: It depends on how one understands the idea of reality.

Joseph: What's that you say?

Pierre: Well, Zeno raises an interesting issue and it is what most people believe. The idea of multiple realities allows for the possibility of many universes, or realities. They cannot think of any reason it could not be so. It actually supports their notion that everything is relative and that there is nothing unique, or so different, as to suggest that its uniqueness makes it superior. If there are different realities, then who is to say that one is superior, or better, than another because each would just be different and not better. This is the hypothesis of the common man, and whether it can withstand scrutiny is the question.

Joseph: Well, can't there be many realities? If so, there would be many different ones out there somewhere and since time and space are unlimited there would be plenty of opportunity for them to come and go, each separate and some like and some unlike another.

Pierre: Perhaps, but let me ask you a question. When you have different realities, or different kinds of anything, do we not ask, "If they are different, yet each and every one is a reality, then must they not share some likeness? For if they did not, how could they be said to be distinguished as being different kinds of reality?"

Joseph: Perhaps and perhaps not.

Pierre: Try this question: "If there are different kinds of color, would not each still have to be a color and so share a fundamental likeness?"

Joseph: Of course.

Pierre: Would not each of the different kinds of color be unlike the others? If not, there would be no point in calling them colors, right? And so on for all things?

Joseph: Sure.

Pierre: So each color would be like another in being a color and unlike in being a different color? And so on for other things?

Joseph: Yes, that's obvious.

Pierre: And if they were all alike in one respect, then in that respect they would be similar to one another? And if they were all unlike one another in another respect, then they would be dissimilar?

Joseph: I think so.

Pierre: Then there is no problem in saying that things can be like and unlike.

Joseph: Interesting. Now what about realities?

Pierre: Well, if they were different kinds of reality, they must be different from one another and yet share something essential in that they belong to the same class. So they would be like and unlike one another?

Joseph: Sure, just like things.

Pierre: And in some respect each of these realities would be the same, or similar, or be like, yet different, dissimilar and not like one another?

Joseph: True enough.

Pierre: Yet they cannot be said to be really different from one another or they would not be in the same class, or subclass, as the other. The greater the difference between anything the less likely they will be in the same class, right?

Joseph: True enough.

Pierre: Nor could these realities be unlike one another if their unlikeness was essential to what they are?

Joseph: True enough.

Pierre: But do you agree that what each reality essentially is must be what is essential to it being reality?

Joseph: Sure thing.

Pierre: But could these realities suffer being like and unlike one another without ceasing to be what they are essentially?

Joseph: No.

Pierre: So if there are many realities each could be contrasted and compared in terms of same, other, like, and unlike?

Joseph: Yes.

Pierre: I wonder if there can be many realities.

Joseph: I thought we agreed that there could be many realities.

Pierre: Perhaps, but if it is not possible for there to be many realities then reality is just what it is. It would be singular and if there were no others, being singular, then it would be impossible to compare and contrast it with other realities since there wouldn't be any. If there were copies or appearances of reality these things could be judged as being either like or unlike.

Joseph: You are saying that realities are not many but one, right?

Pierre: True, for if there were many realities they would have to preserve their essential likeness and unlikeness, but wouldn't this be impossible? For how can essentially different things be said to belong to the same class?

Joseph: I guess it would only be possible if their differences were not essential to their being what they are. I see what you are saying, but it still seems to me like there should be other realities, you know different realities?

Pierre: Well, if so we could ask, "Whenever there are different kinds of anything can we not ask what is the source of this variety?"

Joseph: Sure.

Pierre: Then if there were different realities we would ask how they came to be, would we not?

Joseph: I think so.

Pierre: Well, if we call them all realities they must share something in common, and that sameness must have a cause. For if there are likenesses among the realities, would it not have a source that would be different from those realities?

Joseph: I would say so.

Pierre: However, a source for any manyness of anything would be its cause and that would be its fundamental and essential reality, would it not?

Joseph: I am following, yes.

Pierre: So then the source of the Many would be one?

Joseph: Yes.

Pierre: So would you say that reality is not many, but one?

Joseph: Seems so.

Pierre: Now, the opposite of reality is appearance, is it not? And the appearances of anything are plural, but the source, or reality, is one?

Joseph: Yes. The copies of it could be many, but the source, or model, must be a one.

Pierre: Would you not add that the idea of reality means nothing more basic, or essential, or fundamental has been reached?

Joseph: Yes, again.

Pierre: So when we encounter any manyness we know that not any one of that manyness is the fundamental or essential cause of the manyness.

Joseph: Sure thing.

Pierre: And if there were many realities they would not be the Reality since a manyness is always appearance and its cause would not be among the many realities.

Joseph: Correct.

Pierre: Then is there anyway we can avoid the idea that reality is one and not many?

Joseph: I see the point.

Pierre: Then how could they suffer becoming or being like and unlike one another if there are no plural realities, no manyness to reality? For the fundamental reality of anything cannot be one of the many realities. In this way we would say it is impossible for there to be a manyness, and even if there were they would have to go through what seems to us to be something quite impossible.

Joseph: Seems that way, and this would apply to beings being plural, too.

Pierre: Correct.

Joseph: Actually, I liked the translation that used the idea of things rather than realities. Now it seems I see why you prefer the one that uses reality. You know that if Plato meant reality instead of things, then it does seem to fit the rest of the work better. But who is to say what was on his mind if the same word can be translated in those different ways?

Pierre: If he has the kind of mind that can produce the *Parmenides*, then what do you think?

Joseph: I see what you are saying.

Pierre: If we rise to his level, we can see the way he sees. Insight does spring forth from the mind, doesn't it?

Joseph: I guess I agree. I say that because it seems I had to agree because you frame arguments that force me to accept the idea. It didn't come out of me, you know. If you don't mind my saying so, it is kind of like it jumped out of you fully armed and ready to fight for that conclusion.

Pierre: Interesting image you have there.

Joseph: Say, Pierre, I just thought of something. When Parmenides explores the four hypotheses in which one and many can be discussed, I mean the 2nd, 3rd, 4th, and 5th, do you think those are the ways the One relates to the many realities? Does he not set the first of the four positive ones saying simply of the second: "If One is"; the third as "It is both One-and-Many, and in turn neither One-nor-Many"; the fourth as: "What will happen to the others if One is"; the fifth as: "If One is, whether those other than The One, will not subsist in this way, or whether in this way alone"? and those that follow, the sixth to the ninth, are the rejections of those prior four. Recall the difference between discussing the One itself and the One that exists, or is?

Pierre: Yes I do, and the grounds for rejecting each of them are clearly stated.

Joseph: So he states the four ways as different realities that might exist and shows the grounds for the denials of each?

Pierre: Yes.

Joseph: I am confused. Are there or aren't there four kinds of realities? Since there appears to be, then realities are many and not one, right?

Pierre: Yes, you are right.

Joseph: Then what's going on?

Pierre: You are in a good mood to study just what it is that is Parmenides' hypothesis. Is Plato claiming there are ten, nine, or eight, or only one?

Joseph: I guess you have to study the whole of it and figure it out.

Pierre: The problem Zeno raises is very interesting because it actually is the tenth hypothesis.

Joseph: What? The tenth hypothesis?

Pierre: Zeno introduces his idea that "things are many" as the first hypothesis of his argument and since it is rejected it is one of the hypotheses that are rejected. Each of the others is coherent, consistent, and logically sound, not Zeno's. Zeno's hypothesis has no reference to the One, only to many.

Joseph: Wait a minute, that means Plato does accept that realities are many, or does he?

Pierre: It may seem that way, but what if Parmenides rejects them? What if his hypothesis is "The One," and he offers what follows if one asserts that it is, or is not?

Joseph: I'll have to read that again. You are saying Parmenides only has one hypothesis and that is "if One," right?

Pierre: Right you are about that, and now what if there is one possibility that is missing? What if there could be realities that are not in any way related to the One. By Zeno introducing this possibility he sets the stage for examining whether any set of realities can be without reference to the One.

Joseph: Well, each one would be one.

Pierre: Good point, Joseph. If the second to the fifth hypothesis asserts existence, or being, to each then realities are many. It all depends on a higher question and that is how to understand Parmenides' conclusion.

Joseph: I once heard that argument, but I am not sure if I agree with it or not. If you don't mind, would you give me a recollection of it, or take me through it?

Pierre: Let me start it off by asking a different kind of question, a curious one.

Joseph: Go ahead.

Pierre: If a triangle can be said to exist and if it can be equally and perfectly argued that it does not exist, what would your conclusions be? Or, in general, if arguments for the existence of something are equally as sound as the arguments against the existence of that thing, what conclusion would you draw?

Joseph: One cancels the other out. I guess you could say the triangle neither exists nor does it not exist. If it doesn't exist it might still have some mode of existence other than existence. It could be that it is something we created that has no existence apart from an idea in our minds. I guess you could call it a fiction, a myth, something like a ghost.

Pierre: Then what follows if each of the hypotheses has a counter hypothesis that denies its existence? Further, what if the same conclusion can be made in the summary of all the positive and negative hypotheses?

Joseph: I guess you would say that only the first exists.

Pierre: But, Joseph, suppose the first denies any kind of existence to it?

Joseph: That does it for me. I am not sure where to go with that conclusion. It leaves me blank. Wait a minute! You can still experience a triangle even if it doesn't exist.

Pierre: Since no one can draw a perfect triangle then no one can experience it. The drawn triangle would be an imperfect triangle, and it is this that can be experienced.

Joseph: True, there are things that you can experience even though they are not really real.

Pierre: And let me stress that experience and reason should always be the hallmark of philosophy.

Joseph: In a way I agree and in a way I don't. For me reason has been divorced from experience, and with the dialectic even more so. Let me ask again: What is really philosophically important about these purely dialectical trips? I do get into them for a while, but I always end up feeling entirely unaffected by them because they don't fully relate to me; so I end up feeling somewhat foolish for going along with them—maybe even ignorant though I follow the words.

Pierre: First, it is not easy to see things spiritual and philosophical because you need to know what to look for and what to notice when it is absent. It is not easy, but it is worth the effort. It simply takes time to cultivate an understanding of what to look for. Once you become sensitive to what is there it becomes obvious that it has been there all along.

You cultivate an understanding of key ideas, and then let things take their natural course. Understanding prepares the mind for vision, and to nurture its development it needs only your kind attention. Curiously enough this brings with it a way of understanding that has an enduring presence that creates a foundation for being more oneself than before.

Joseph: If I put that description in my mind and walk around with it, then do you think it will make me more sensitive to the idea itself?

Pierre: Try it and see. Master the idea; grasp it so thoroughly that you don't have to think about it; leave yourself open, and the practice is what I have just described.

Whatever you study brings you to see more than those who do not study the same thing. What do you say to this? Those who study painting become more sensitive to colors, those who become musicians hear sounds in a different way than those not attuned to sounds, and those who study the way they think and seek to grasp why random thoughts are not random are likely to be more keenly aware of thoughts and images that present themselves to our minds.

Joseph: Sounds right.

Pierre: Then would you go along with the idea that if someone were to make a study of the most fundamental systems of thought, they would be the ones who would be more likely to find similarities between them than others who ignore these things?

Joseph: Then you do think that is what is behind works like the *Parmenides*, don't you? I have heard more than once that these works are, most likely, merely logical exercises. They are logical, yet I can't get anything good out of them, and, curiously, they leave me thinking all this is random words strung together to appear as if they are really linked, but it's only logic that glues it together. I have had a beer over this with some friends and I laughing—claiming this work is the most indefinite definite work there is. They chuckled over my uncoordinated wobbling out of the pub. You hold out and say it is worth the effort to master it, right?

Pierre: Yes, and the mastery of such ideas is the study and mastery of the dialectic.

Joseph: Could you give me an example? What ideas could you use for this?

Pierre: Soul, likeness, intelligible, rest, Providence and others.

Joseph: I have no idea of what Providence means, and few people I know ever use the word. It is just outside my own experience, and what else am I to use to judge it? Once in a while I may have heard the word, Providence, but I let it roll off into the emptiness of the nonsensical. Actually, I would like to say that among terms this one really doesn't work, so it's nonproductive; there is no way it relates to me; it is out of my orbit, if you know what I mean. It is really the same for the four positive ways Parmenides presents the One-Many problem.

Is there any way to make that relate to anything of interest to me? Sure it is a logical exercise, but is it anything else?

Pierre: That's good, anything else?

Joseph: Yes, it is like a dried up riverbed that once overflowed its banks. So I'll tell you what I would like you to do. Take this idea of Providence and treat it dialectically. Wait a minute! Don't take me through an endless set of questions. Can't you just state it all at once? Or isn't that fair to ask?

Pierre: Yes, it is fair. Actually, I do have an interesting statement of one of these ideas with me, and I'll read it and you tell me what idea it is. How does that sound?

Joseph: Is this a bit of fun? Go ahead and read it.

Pierre: Well, now here it is: A pervasive power extends continuously over all, bringing with it a vastly profound goodness that reaches everywhere, it has an awesome effective capability that reaches into the very nature of all things, and as it spreads its wondrous influence it reveals that in its very nature it is goodness. All welcomes her and none would seek to avoid her presence since the will that directs her never deviates from her goal. Here we have a oneness, yet we can say we must acknowledge that guiding all she is not one. Those who receive the benefits of her reign recognize that the extending rays of goodness preserve the richness already received, guiding each throughout its existence, for what guides all from the alpha to the omega of its existence brings all to its measured perfection. She watches over all and can never be said to harm, nor does she bring anything unexpected into the sphere of a splendid order and harmony.

Thus, while it is present to all, it is from another dimension that she transcends those influenced by her, smilingly knowing in one way, but not in another. The influence she has reaches deeply into others, and they, in relating to one another, neither suffer nor experience any injustice that can occur randomly. Bringing all together as if in one single family she closes the door to chance. Naturally, all become good to the degree appropriate to their vision. In one sweep all turn to her for protection, depend upon her goodness, and all benefit by the unending flow that brings all to perfection. Each neither has a freedom to dwell in her spirit nor does any oppose her or rebel against her. For each partakes of her as much as their growth permits and they share in her magnanimous gifts as they ascend into the destiny that lies for Man far beyond any fated existence.

Joseph: Now if that were true, it is what I'd call something ideally good. Wait a minute. Why are you folding up and putting that paper away so fast? Come on let me see that paper you are reading. Come on now! Were you pretending to read it?

Pierre: I'll show it after you tell me what idea it is.

Joseph: I don't know, maybe Soul, Intelligence, or Being.

Pierre: It is a word that is prior to the intellect, prior to the intelligible, it is a goodness that flows from the Good itself and is called, in English, Providence. I presented it in the spirit of the dialectic. What is here is its positive mode, and it also has a parallel to what could be said about it if it were not functioning. If you look at it closely you will see that it defines what it is in itself, what it reigns over, its influence among others relating to each other, and how each can be said to relate to its source. It is the same for the ordering of the four positive and negative hypotheses in the *Parmenides*. Yet, for all this analysis remember that the word describes what truly is and to realize that it takes paying attention in a most curious way. We are not taught to study states of mind nor how to develop a way of understanding based upon the way a thing functions. To grasp Providence is to learn to see with the eye of the soul.

Joseph: So that is the practice of being thoughtfully watchful.

Pierre: Yes, practice is keeping it in mind as you look out on the world and on yourself. You caught an aspect of the central idea when you just said that it is being thoughtfully watchful.

Joseph: What am I missing? I would like to hear about it since it must be what you need to see Providence, and I do like the way you just described it. What do you say? Or is it another Greek word that we lack a corresponding term for? Am I going to have to dig, search, and get confused looking for something I don't understand?

Pierre: Well, it is no easy task you are setting for both of us, Joseph. As for me I would appreciate, if you don't mind, if we set this issue aside because it will involve us in a long discussion that I just may not have the energy, power, or time to work through at this time. So shall we set it aside as something I owe you that you might collect at sometime in the future?

Joseph: No. But I will ask you to include in the talk why it would take so much more from you than what you freely engage in.

Pierre: Perhaps, it is also because we have enough before us to explore and for us to jump into another subject might make us akin to those hungry eaters who devour one plate of food after another before they have fully tasted and digested what they have already eaten.

Joseph: That may be true because my mind does bring me back to an issue we nibbled on. We were moving along with the idea that it is possible to be religious without faith, and that is something I am very interested in exploring.

Pierre: Yes, there is something important in what you say, Joseph. However, it is often the case that one can be religious without having a spiritual life, and have a spiritual life without being connected to any religion. Religion binds people together under a belief that is believed to be a saving power. It does not require the believer to discover meaning nor to practice a discipline for reaching more profound states of Being, or mind.

The spiritual is to use the mind to see the mind and in reaching beyond it to recognize its source. It is a way, a journey, along a much-fabled way to gain freedom from fate in embracing one's destiny. To be fated is to carry on with what has already been learned from one's early years, and destiny is to break out of those bonds and be what we are here to be. The religious way is to use belief to feel secure about one's fate and expect and put one's hope in the realization that comes after death.

Joseph: You know what? I never saw that before but Providence and grace are really different. For you it fits into reality, but for me I will just have to see.

You are saying that this idea of Providence that you just read is actually a dialectical treatment of the idea. Interesting it is. I guess you could put it out as a set of questions and take someone through it. What a trip that would be.

I have to admit this is an interesting way to explore an idea, but for all that I wonder how it fits into the One-Many problem. I think I see it and then it slips away. Would you take me through what you see about it?

Pierre: Would you take an analogy as an answer?

Joseph: Right now I would take anything.

Pierre: The One is to the Many as Providence is to its effects. The Good is to goodness as goodness is to Providence.

Joseph: I'll have to consider that for a while.

Pierre: When you do you recollect that the Good is more magnificent than goodness as any cause is greater than its effects. Consider the primal cause as one thing, and recall that that without which a cause could not be a cause is far greater in depth and power, so the goodness that Providence expresses is far beyond its sublime effects as the Good itself must be to goodness itself.

Joseph: So the One-Many problem expresses that relationship, and I guess you would make the same claim for all the ideas, the metaphysical ideas of this Platonic tradition. So you think these hypotheses in the *Parmenides* may actually fit situations, structures, and systems? If so, then it would be the foundation of them all. Now, that is interesting.

Pierre: What do you find interesting about that?

Joseph: Actually, I just had an insight. If these hypotheses of Parmenides were foundational then what kinds of things would they ideally represent? Like among all systems, which set of ideas have you found them useful for?

Pierre: I enjoy using them to understand different religions and the arguments against them. It is also possible to identify them with the principle philosophies or spiritual systems.

Joseph: Which religions would fit?

Pierre: Those that see the divine interweaving with the cosmos, those that focus on time as the medium through which the divine and the cosmos unfold, those that define themselves as separate and distinct from others, and those transcendental dualistic systems. You could easily place Taoism, Shaivism, Judaic-Christian-Islamic systems, and the transcendental dualistic systems within the second, third, fourth, and fifth hypotheses respectively.

Joseph: I need to see that. What you are saying is that it is possible to study religions without bothering to see their spiritual side. No, you are saying the foundations of each can be seen in Plato's *Parmenides*—wait a minute—which means that Plato laid out the foundations for each before they took on their historical form. Well, maybe some had a rudimentary form before, but as systems this set it out cold for all to see before they came to birth. Now, that is fantastically curious.

Pierre: The hypotheses exhaust the possibilities, don't they?

Joseph: Yes, indeed, he covers all the bases, doesn't he? I like that way of proceeding because it leaves nothing out. Dialectic marches on.

Pierre: Yes, and the model of the *Parmenides'* dialectical approach is set forth in the Plato's *Philebus*.

Joseph: The triad adds another, the fourth. And it becomes a set of four.

Pierre: Yes, and what is it you are puzzling through now?

Joseph: I was just wondering what would it be like for someone to find their own religion identified as one among these many? Like what would it mean? I guess that they would have to see it as merely one among many; none can claim to have a privileged unique place. I wonder if it might disillusion them to know that.

Pierre: They are a part of a whole that they do not understand. However, if they were to discover and understand the nature of that whole, they might reflect that something binds the whole together that is worthy of their attention.

Joseph: Very true.

Pierre: And would you add that it might benefit them to know that the whole of the four parts and their denials is not Parmenides' hypothesis?

Joseph: It is not?

Pierre: You might want to check it out for yourself. It is rather important to know.

Joseph: I'll do that later. Now, if I am not mistaken you are saying that a dialectical study of religions will show that the foundation of all major religions was identified before they were born, can be studied intellectually, and without the necessity of dealing with their spiritual side. No, I guess you are saying the spiritual side had to wait for the historical necessity to appear. So each came into existence when they took on a historical form through the manifestation of the persons who identify and personify them. It makes a kind of sense, the kind you can wonder about.

Pierre: Add to that another point. Those we can call sages, or the holiest of men, or as some call them, heretics, added to the depth of their respective religions. They are the one's whose writings many seek out to read and contemplate since they open the doorway into the mind and the spiritual life. If you take up any of the writings of Pseudo-Dionysius, Shankara, Meister Eckhart, Thomas Aquinas, Al-Farabi, Surwardi, Alexander the Jew, and other sages you will find they included within their writings ideas from the other hypotheses than their own. They found a way to reach beyond the boundary of their system and embrace ideas that bring the most profound insights into themselves and the divine. Within each of their own systems is always the Idea of the Good and the Good itself, or the One. Each of the sages pushed beyond the boundary of their system to include elements that would not merely enhance their system but bring it more akin to the highest realization, the One itself. There are even sages like Simon the theologian who clearly are Parmenidean and yet stay within the system, speak as if it has always been a part of their system, and keep silent about the significance of what they have added.

Joseph: You left out Buddhism, you know. I studied it, too. The Mahayana school, or Northern school, fits the first hypothesis, doesn't it? Their idea of emptiness as the final end is just like the first hypothesis' "that about which you cannot say anything and not even that", right?

Pierre: Yes, that is so.

Joseph: What about Taoism, don't they include the idea of the One, too?

Pierre: Yes, indeed they do. When Taoism is expressed that way it resembles Buddhism's way, as in that the old quote, "The real way is not difficult. It only abhors choice and attachment."

Joseph: There is a lot of richness in that tradition. If they are among the highest, why are we playing around with the second best? If Buddhism can include Taoism why not stay with them?

Pierre: They ignore the mystery of existence, they have no insight into the purpose of existence, and they have no logos, no reason; what they leave behind is the role of Mind. The Platonist includes both the One and the most brilliant light of Being, and the way to reach that is through the cultivation of understanding and the logos, and a curious application of reason. The practice is itself a kind of contemplation and ends in contemplation.

Joseph: Yes, and they have no idea of justice and beauty, do they?

Pierre: Justice includes within itself the idea of righteousness. To realize the necessity for righteousness as the central idea in the spiritual learning of man means that one has fully grasped that goodness is reflected throughout the cosmos and that we are part of a just and providential cosmos. To reach enlightenment and not to understand this is a strange, blank, and empty enlightenment.

Joseph: Now, I do like hearing that and that is pretty heavy. However, I don't recall where Plato describes the Good and the Idea of the Good together, or as it is also called, the One and the most brilliant light of Being. Can you recall or recollect it for me?

Pierre: Here I am having coffee and you want me to work. Well, maybe I will help you, but it is not an easy thing to see, many people can read it, and not see it. Plato makes you work and in the work you come to see just what it takes to understand. What you are inquiring about is expressed in the mean analogy: as the Good is to the Idea of the Good so too the Idea of the Good is to the Sun. When you search it out remember that there are two classes of royal ruling—King and Queen—one of the Divine and the other of the Earthly realm, and please note that the most brilliant light of Being gives birth to the Sun. It is the final stage to the allegory of the cave and the upper world.

Joseph: I appreciate that. So thanks. However, I have to admit that I can't recall that king and queen idea in the *Republic*. I am not even sure that I heard of it, but it sure is a grand idea. Where can I look it up?

Pierre: It is not often discussed as it should be; that's for sure. It is the high point in the allegory of the cave and the upper world after he discusses the "last of all to be known." Plato writes in such a way that you have to be careful to construct what he only hints at; it forces the readers to puzzle out these ideas and see for themselves. It is the union of the highest and most profound of Platonic ideas.

Joseph: This stuff interests me and I always wanted to explore it with you, so thanks again. When I studied Zen Buddhism, they called thinking a sickness of the mind and insisted we banish all thoughts. I am attracted to Plato because the very game of dialogue says the rational is to be cultivated, not denied. The Buddhist game, as I understood it, was to pull away from all experience, a kind of rejection of whatever is happening; it was a practice of detaching yourself from whatever you experience. I got bored with it, and since I couldn't drop the boredom I kind of dropped out of Buddhism. I learned to breathe though.

Originally I was attracted to Tibetan Buddhism, but ended up with Zen because of some Zen Masters I had heard about and admired. Now, I would like to ask you about something I heard about. You had a talk with Lama Govinda. Those who reported it didn't have what I would call a good recollection, and I would really like to know from you what it was about.

Pierre: It wasn't much of a talk. I had studied the *Tibetan Book of the Dead* and *Milarepa* with Lama Tada back in the 50s, and we talked about this very issue. Lama Anagarika Govinda wrote one of the introductions to Evans Wentz' translation of the *Tibetan Book of the Dead*. I had the chance to ask him at a public session about the state of perfect enlightenment, the Dharma Kaya, the Body of Truth. It is claimed to be the union of pure consciousness, as being void, and the intellect, shining blissfully. I raised that idea because, as I reasoned, if the perfect state is a union of these two, then it is not empty.

When Lama Govinda caught the significance of the question he lost his cool and directed his anger at me and insisted I was absurd to think that. I mentioned he could find that idea on page 96 in the very book he had written the commentary on, and that did it, the lecture ended. The reason for my question was that I wanted to understand if that union I just described was like that Divine Royalty mentioned in Plato's *Republic*.

Joseph: Well thanks; I now have a good recollection. How does that relate to the Parmenidean hypotheses?

Pierre: If that idea of the union could be said, then the Tibetan Buddhist tradition had a work that could include both the first and second Hypotheses, so that idea it is not only found in Plato and the Platonic tradition.

I have since learned that subsequent translations have not included this idea, so it is fair to say that there is a good deal at stake over this idea. For myself, I wonder if they reached that idea of the union why they didn't develop as the Platonic tradition did.

Joseph: I think I see what you are saying. You are arguing for the inclusion of these philosophical ideas within each system. The union of the sages, I'd call it. You know, of course, that it will make them Platonic.

Pierre: It is true that those in the Platonic tradition always make room for further insights and rejoice when they find another who can shed light on the mystery of our existence and the divine.

Joseph: What might that mean to them to bring this into their system?

Pierre: They can preserve their traditions and infuse it with that which was the cause of their systems.

Joseph: And, Pierre, does the Platonic tradition gain anything by all the contrasting and comparing itself with these other spiritual systems? If so, would Plato liked to have seen it, too?

Pierre: Let's explore an idea my way, if you don't mind a bit of fun. First off, would you agree that a warrior, or someone in the martial arts, would appreciate learning to develop a state of mind that would allow them to act with the full force of their being in the most unexpected situations, without having to plan or think out whatever they do, and for their acts to be entirely appropriate to whatever circumstances they encounter? The acts would flow freely with a power most can only dream of possessing; and while functioning in this way, they would be in command of themselves and of the scenes in which they play a most significant part.

Joseph: Indeed, a Samurai warrior in that state would be the envy of his clan. His acts would naturally flow with the spirit of equanimity and freedom. The art that develops this state of mind is the ideal among Zen Buddhists.

Pierre: Now, what if one could seize upon that state and develop its power in order to turn the soul around to face the most brilliant light of Being, the Idea of the Good?

Joseph: Are you saying this is in Plato? In Plato's *Republic*?

Pierre: Try something for me. You know Barbara Stecker, don't you? Well, she has made a word search of a certain Greek word and can identify every occurrence of this word as well as its opposite. She shared with me the list of some 100 references. What if all these references cluster around this one term we just discussed in Zen? What if those who most fully possess this state of mind are the only ones who are selected for the full training of the philosopher king?

Joseph: And my friend Socrates was said to have distinguished himself as a warrior who could be only lightly clad and walk through the snow without leggings or shoes, could meditate standing on one spot for 24 hours, and drink everyone under the table. I like him. I will check with Barbara and do that very thing.

What word is it in Zen? I guess I should know, but I forgot it, I guess. Oh, and what is the Greek word?

Pierre: In Zen it is *"joriki,"* and in the Greek it is *"phronasis."*

Joseph: You are right about that, Pierre, because joriki is not enlightenment, or satori, and curiously enough, it too needs a more profound practice or learning to advance to enlightenment. You know that I have enjoyed reflecting that both the Zen master and the philosopher return to the everyday pursuits of man to fully realize their enlightenment. Did you know that they call that final stage *"mujodo no taigen,"* an actualization of their vision in the everyday world?

Pierre: Yes, indeed, and the delightful image of the tenth Ox-herding picture captures the final stage of that spiritual quest most exquisitely, "Without recourse to mystic powers, withered trees he swiftly brings to bloom." And in the allegory of the cave, the philosopher who returns from the upper world is like Socrates purging those false ideas of justice of those around him and challenging them to enter the practice of true philosophy and gain a vision of the Idea of the Good and the Good itself. That kind of vision and understanding affords the philosopher the verification that Providence of the divine can be seen in the everyday world, that the spiritual path that leads to it is similar to that in other spiritual systems, and the cultivation of phronasis is essential to that path.

Joseph: Are you having fun at my expense again, Pierre? Go ahead. I see what you have done. This is the debt you owed, right?

Pierre: I do guess you could say I may have paid it off sufficiently. *The Republic* builds a very careful case that this power is already in the soul, and it only needs an art to focus it rather than as it usually is done: dissipate it thoughtlessly. Once unified it can be used to turn the soul around to its proper object, the Idea of the Good and the Good itself. What does one then see but that we live in an intelligible cosmos that seeks in every way to benefit us? By developing this complementary art, we experience, see, and understand that Providence flows freely to all who are open to accept her.

Joseph: If this is so, and it seems to me now that it might very well be true, then it is worth it to study Plato alongside of other spiritual systems. I see why you say that spiritual systems are never at war with one another, nor seek to out do one another, but they can benefit by mutual sharing, right?

Pierre: There is only one mind, one mind we participate in, one human fellowship. What does that mean? To some, at least those with mind, they will see there is little need to war against others since the others can reflect the highest vision too. They can be part of a spiritual awakening by awakening to the divine that is causeless yet is everywhere being reflected in all.

Joseph: A new band of brothers, it is.

Pierre: Yes, indeed, and those who can participate in this are drawn to the Progressive Theology of the One while those who stay within their historical boundaries can be said to be guided by Conservative Theology.

Joseph: The strange thing is that I have known ministers who do not seem to me to be in any way concerned with the spiritual dimension we spoke about. I imagine that they are members of the Conservative Theology.

Pierre: Well, even though you do not believe in God, or the Good, you can still want to be a shepherd over your flock. It does have advantages and power.

Joseph: For me, I have often thought that there is a single idea that is shared by all these religious systems and that is the fear of death. Each of them offers the same hope that in death they will be saved. All they believe will be confirmed after death. They are religions of death and they expect their followers to believe that belief alone will overcome their stark fear of death. Nothing philosophical there, is there?

Pierre: No, none at all. Philosophy is nothing other than the study and practice of death. For the true philosopher death is the separation of the soul from the body, and the practice of philosophy is to master just how to separate one's soul from the body before you drop dead and are buried.

Joseph: I don't recall where that is in Plato, but I am sure you are right.

Pierre: Good heavens, Joseph, do you want to become a believer? I don't know what to do with you.

Joseph: I goofed, you're right. I would like to hear it again, or read it, later.

Pierre: Platonic philosophy is a spiritual system and has what we would today call yoga; it is jñana yoga, wisdom yoga. The practice of death is a meditation, a continual practice, which is purification because it prepares the soul to make the separation and partake of the realm of Being. Here now, reflect on a passage from Plato's *Phaedo*,

> "And is not purification really that which has been mentioned so often in our discussion, to separate as far as possible the soul from the body, and to accustom it to collect itself together out of the body in every part, and to dwell alone by itself as far as it can, both at this present and in the future, being freed from the body as if from a prison."[2]

Joseph: Thanks, that is a nice recollection. It sounds like it was from Rouse's translation? I would like to review it carefully. Say, did Balboa do a *Phaedo* translation? I'll bet comparing his translation with Rouse would really be fun. Then comparing them with the Thomas Taylor's would be a delight. It is likely that Juan Balboa has compared them all, isn't it?

Pierre: He will be at our usual Friday night talk; you might ask him about it.

Joseph: Did I ever mention that when I studied philosophy at the university, my professor insisted that Socrates' argument for the existence of the soul was a pure case of nonsense?

Pierre: I have heard that tale from others. It is what you can expect from those who have been only taught to defend science, common sense, and some form of Empiricism. Those who are drawn to study these topics are not those who have a natural affinity with the Platonic tradition. It is the same problem with psychology because those drawn to behaviorism are hardly those attracted to Carl Jung and Socratic midwifery. The study of the Platonic tradition challenges and attracts a different kind of person, not Aristotelians.

Joseph: You might find Platonists in heaven, but there are few in the school system.

Pierre: The persistence of an anti-Platonic spirit in academia is the problem. These texts of the Platonic tradition are so profound that they challenge the myths of scholarship and culture. It takes courage to see what these texts are saying, it challenges the myth of progress, and all contemporary religions would be threatened by making them the major object of enquiry.

Joseph: I think it comes down to the issue of what is education. I guess there has to be a public debate about the goal of education, and around that problem there is going to be plenty of conflict.

Pierre: It is a sad and troublesome problem. We do not appreciate the difference between learning and teaching. When you are told something, repeat it, write it out, then you have been taught. Following a line of reasoning, thinking it out for yourself, coming to your own conclusion, demonstrating, and applying, is learning.

Joseph: That fits much of my education and nails some of my old professors right on the head.

Pierre: The name professor says it all because it was coined to define the role of the teacher. Whenever a student's faith is threatened by some ideas in a text, the professor stands, as it were, between the student and text and defends or interprets the text to save the faith and dispel doubt.

Joseph: The church did play a role in all that, didn't it?

Pierre: Yes, that was an edict back in 1270 issued for the University of Paris, called by some the Averroes heresy; it blocked the idea that truth could be found simply by allowing readers to study the philosophical texts by themselves and be guided only by logic. Universities created the idea of the professor to defend the faith by insisting that they interject interpretations of a text to save the faith.

Joseph: Curious it is that faith and reason, education and learning, and science and metaphysics may really spin around this strange idea of death. If the central idea of the Platonic tradition is this idea of a philosophical death then it challenges the religious beliefs of our society. If we agree to avoid it, then it preserves those who have most to lose by an open educational system.

Pierre: Yes, that is where it goes.

Joseph: So simply skip that idea of death; interpret it away. But what if a Platonist was exploring that idea of death? Would he not say that if you have any questions about what is said, a better reading of it would solve the problem? And if they wanted to know if it were true, or if the soul could be separated from the body, I do imagine he would say try it and see.

Pierre: And what do you think would follow if they advanced and encouraged that idea of a philosophical death?

Joseph: Well, you couldn't put Platonic yoga in the university; it wouldn't be allowed. Horrors to be. Say, Pierre, what is it like when the soul is separated from the body?

Pierre: The same terms that Plato uses to describe Being are those he uses to describe the state of the soul separated from the body.

Joseph: The idea of Being returns, again. Little wonder that the university system is anti-Platonic. Can you imagine what it would be like to add the Platonic tradition to the school system? They would have to study analogy, allegory, symbols, mythology, love, and mention the need to master contemplation, dialectic, theurgy and theology. Empiricists and logical positivists would run down the halls screaming they have been betrayed.

Pierre: Good point there, Joseph. These logical positivists have been nursed on a watered down brew of Plato. It has been poured down their throats by their own gentleman's agreement not to look into the mysticism of Plato. When they do read Plato they believe they are finding fault with his thought, but their arguments are as shallow as their mythical view of Plato. They fail to grasp what anyone who knows Plato knows, and that is simply that an idea is no more a concept than a positivist is a philosopher. So as it is often said, "You can led a logical positivist to Plato, but you can't make him think."

The problem is an old one. It is a simple, but higher issue. It comes down to, "What does it take to read?" For the persistence of an anti-Platonic spirit in academia is called by some of our friends the Jacob Klein problem. These texts of the Platonic tradition are so profound that they challenge the myths of scholarship and culture. It takes courage to see what these texts are saying. It challenges the myth of progress, and all contemporary religions would be threatened by making them the major object of enquiry.

Joseph: I don't recall the Klein problem. Is it in some strange way a religious problem?

Pierre: No, unless it functioned on a deeper level. You see, Klein could read it, he understood the Greek, but couldn't grasp the idea of the philosophical death being a yoga.

Joseph: I do wish I understood that in some deeper way. It has to do with seeing, or willing to see, or the refusal to see.

Pierre: Yes, the idea of death is for Plato an experience, and he urges us to gain that experience before we drop dead. The nature of Being is no small puzzle. The separation of the soul from the body is a purification that brings the vision of Being itself.

Joseph: Well, well, we are back with my old problem with Being.

Pierre: Let's try exploring it. You did say that your idea of Being, or Beings, is not at all clear to you. Let me suggest something and you tell me which word would fit this idea. There is an experience called divine luminosity, a divine radiance, the pure light of Being, the most brilliant light of Being, and it is also said to be pure, everlasting, immortal and unchanging.

Joseph: A mystical state, clearly, yet not alien to reason.

Pierre: Clearly this magnificent and profound experience brings with it the astonishing claim that it is something that truly is, and is the utmost real, or Reality; therefore, it has been called Truth. Now the one word that covers all these expressions is Being.

Joseph: So that is what is behind that word. I never put those two things together. I wonder why?

Pierre: You have the right question.

Joseph: That was very helpful. It certainly is not a thing, or some everyday thing, that exists or has existence. Now Pierre, would I be pushing too hard if I were to ask another personally curious but important question? Everyone around here may know what is meant by the idea of the One; it is often spoken about. Yet for all the talk, I wonder if there is anything to it that links it with the spiritual realm. Sure. I know that God is One and all that, but is there something I am missing about it because it still leaves me cold? Is there something about it that I am missing, or is it simply like the saying that God is One?

Pierre: What you are asking is simple; how to answer it is not. If you were to ask the question in terms of a philosophical or metaphysical cosmology, we could use Proclus' *Elements*, the thirteenth proposition. Let me use the theologian we mentioned earlier, Simon. He is speaking in the Parmenidean tradition when he says,

> "Who is blind to the One, is completely blind to all. Who sees the One, has vision of all—and at any rate is removed from their vision, and in the vision of all becomes, and outside of all he is. Inside the

One he sees everything, and while being in everything nothing of any thing does he see."

Whoever sees in the One through the One, sees clearly himself and all men and all things, and hidden inside the One, he doesn't see anything of any thing.

Joseph: Well, I do see that you have to carry that around with you. Very fine statement; I am going to look into it. If I get what you are saying it seems that all these spiritual seekers you just mentioned would all understand one another, wouldn't they?

Joseph: Yes, they would share the same language even though they might stress this or that aspect of it.

Pierre: Then this shared language has the same goal; and while it is expressed most profoundly in Plato, it is a common language to describe and explain the spiritual life of Man. Within the scope of philosophy, then, there stands the most brilliant light of Being and the Good, or the One. The idea of Being often gives readers a difficulty because behind that one word, Being, in the Greek there are two.

Joseph: Now, that I would like to hear about.

Pierre: The other word is the other side of the idea of Being. So then let me ask you: what shall we call something that reverts upon itself, eternally seeing itself, and in turning upon itself it furnishes its own being, so that needing nothing it is akin to the One itself, but not the One?

Joseph: What do you mean by that idea? Is it derived from something that must logically be said, or is it possible that it is experience? If it is experienced, can it be seen to match your description?

Pierre: Those who have experienced Being know what it is, and it can be known in a brief experience that seems timeless and real. But those who have experienced it more fully and have been able to describe what it is know that it is *ousia*.

These are the ones who realized that in shedding even the slightest hint of a mask, the most minuscule tension, or dropping even the idea of dropping, what is encountered is a deeper vision of the vibrant luminosity that becomes more profoundly what it is, so it is easy to say that it knows itself knowing and in that knowing is self creating. Hence, *ousia* is defined as that which turns upon itself, is seeing itself, and is self-creating.

Joseph: And, The Good is beyond that!

Pierre: The most brilliant light of Being is a beatific experience, and recall that "to behold" is what the Greek word "idea" means. It is not merely a concept, and since the idea of beholding the Good is an experience, a beatific experience, it gives, or shares, with those who experience it the very power of knowing itself. However, since whatever is must have a cause, then that which most fully is must have a cause. So that most splendid Idea of the Good, beholding the Good, must have a cause; and it is this that transcends it as it also does knowledge and all knowing, for intellect cannot reach what lies beyond its grasp.

Joseph: It is a remarkable idea. I just wonder if this kind of reflection dethrones the Intellect.

Pierre: Yes, you have something important there. For there are many who have trained themselves to become objects of adoration by training and sharpening their thinking to secure for themselves places of honor and authority and they call this intellectual training, but it is a far cry from liberating the Intellect so that it can be brought to vision.

Joseph: The Klein problem surfaces again. Then they neither gain true knowledge of the idea of the Good nor even understand the Good itself. Curious it is. The vision of the very nature of Reality, of Being itself, must be the greatest of all experiences. I have heard you say that it comes to those to whom it comes by contemplation, in dreams, by fasting, and, for some through LSD. It must be the crowning experience, must it not?

Pierre: Yes it is, and from it can you see that one can derive the five principle ideas: Being, Same, Other, Motion, and Rest? The experience is of Being: as it unfolds it can be said to have some kind of divine Motion and yet in remaining itself, it is at Rest; and in remaining the Same while showing a deeper aspect of itself in its very dynamic, it can also be said to have Otherness.

Joseph: So the word includes both an experiential side, and from it a logical set of inferences. Meaning needs both, and they form a perfect union, don't they?

Pierre: True it is. It is a wondrous word, *ousia*, for which we have no generally agreed upon English equivalent, and some don't believe it necessary to coin a new word for it. Balboa's translation always uses the word essence for that key word. Many translators substitute the word Being for it.

Joseph: No wonder there is some confusion. Hurrah for the Balboa translation. Say, he did the Proclus' *Elements of Theology* didn't he?

Pierre: Yes, and a good one it is.

Joseph: There is more to do isn't there? I ask that because I do have a few puzzles myself.

Pierre: Sure thing. Now we will explore what the One is, what relation there can be between the One and the Many, and if it is possible for there to be such relationships.

Joseph: Yes, I see where this is going. After all this talk I still wonder about why the Ancient Greeks expressed devotion to their Gods and Goddesses. Would you mind returning to that issue?

Pierre: The question about the Gods and Goddess is important to reflect upon, Joseph. However, before answering your query, I have another question to ask you. Do you think that we live in a cosmos where it is possible to use the mind to know the mind; is it possible that there is a proper place in our traditions for the dialectic, and for the love of wisdom, or philosophy? Is it worth reflecting on? Is it worthy of respect? Should we acknowledge the presence of these things? If we acknowledge and honor what made these things an essential essence of our cosmos, then might we personify these essences and call them Gods and Goddesses?

Joseph: To grant that much to the ancients means they saw better than we do. They recognized and honored what we dismiss. I guess I would have to say that I find that very interesting, indeed.

Pierre: I think I can match your curiosity, Joseph. I do think I have a recollection of a part of a lost play that only recently was recovered that had a reference to Athena. While it is short you might find it worth reflecting over, even though I can't quite recall the opening lines.

> "…Gray-eyed Athena
> Sprung forth from the forehead of Mighty Zeus unaided;
> for Mind as it is in itself brings forth Wisdom, unaided,
> expressing that fullest flowering of itself,
> for the image of the spear merely pointed
> to the sudden power of the birth."

Joseph: Yes, I do find that attractive and there is something about it that strikes me as true. However, I think I can match your recollection with one of my own. You see, I just had a recollection of that discussion we just had about Providence. Now tell me: Is there also a negative side to it, one that would show if there was none? I mean if there wasn't Providence or if there was Providence, but it didn't or couldn't function?

Pierre: I do think that you are a quick learner; however, Joseph, the negatives have been cited, and you know it very well.

Joseph: I do? Where?

Pierre: You have been living it. You just might take a look and see.

Joseph: You mean, don't you, in this very dialogue? I guess you do.

Pierre: Well, it is time for me to go and for you to reflect. Here is the paper you asked about.

Joseph: What? It's blank.

References

[1] Plato with an English Translation, *Parmenides*, H. N. Fowler. Harvard University Press, ©1963, p. 203, 127E-128A.

[2] Great Dialogues of Plato, *Phaedo*, Translated by W.H.D. Rouse. Edited by Eric Warmington and Philip G. Rouse, Signet Classic, printed 1999. ©1956, 1984 by John Cline Graves Rouse. p. 470, (67B).

"The idea of likeness is a principle idea in metaphysics. The study of metaphysics requires that you allow yourself to explore ideas in a new way. It is said to be simple and difficult. Simple because if you reflect each of the points in a metaphysical exploration they should be simple. But the simple for the wise may not be the simple for the fool. The fool's simplicity might become wise if he would endure the study of the simple, but the fool's foolishness is in believing that doing that is foolish."

Pierre Grimes, *Is It All Relative?* p.124.

Hellenism and Madhyamika Buddhism: A Dialogue on the Dialectic

Raymond: Greetings Joseph. Well, you and I both made time for a talk over coffee, and this is a good place. There isn't much business at this time so we can sit back and get into those issues that we agreed to discuss in your e-mail. I don't have to tell you that they are important to me, so when I heard you make a distinction last Friday night between religion and having a spiritual life, I knew you were going to launch into an interesting discussion; and I wanted to hear all about it.

Joseph: That's right. Either one doesn't necessarily entail the other. You can be religious without having a spiritual life and have a spiritual life without being religious. On the one hand religion binds people together under one belief and that, in some way, satisfies their religious needs; but on the other hand one's spiritual life is rooted in personal experience that transcends belief and everyday worldly experiences. As for the discussion you were referring to, I remember that you didn't say much at the time.

Raymond: Well, the views you presented were so new and since it opened up a whole new area for me to explore, I didn't want to say anything before that group until I got into it further. Now, I'm aware that scholarship can impact one's understanding of religious movements, but it never dawned on me that it might cause someone like myself to be turned around as much as it has. I can't get over it. The idea that scholarship can uncover the origin of major religious movements and in doing so awaken philosophy to explore its own spiritual roots sounded so weird I had to look into it. As I wrote you in my e-mail, I've been involved in Zen Buddhism, but I'm still drawn to all that Platonic stuff that you introduced me to through those Golden West College philosophy courses. So I came running when I heard that you were exploring the links between Madhyamika Buddhism and Plato because that sounded so strange and unlikely that I wanted to hear from you what you found.

Joseph: When I e-mailed you back, I cited those books and articles we discussed that day; and from what I hear I assume you must have gotten into them. I would really like to know what you found significant and insightful in them.

Hellenism and Madhyamika Buddhism: A Dailogue on the Dialectic

Raymond: I opened with Thomas McEvilley's stuff. His view of Plotinus was very insightful, and he really showed how similar it is to Vijnanavada Buddhism. I sure liked the way he saw those two ways of viewing Plotinus' thought as both an ontological and idealist viewpoint. I always like seeing such parallels between systems, but when I got into his Pyrrhonism and the Madhyamika Buddhism, that did it for me. I'd like to go over a few things he said about Nagarjuna because my own Zen Buddhism comes out of his school and was shaped by it. But I have to tell you that I never would have thought that Pyrrhonism was introduced into India at the time of Alexander the Great. From what I read his entourage included Pyrrhon, his master Anxarchus, and the Cynic philosopher, Onesicritus. Are you satisfied that there is some archeological evidence to support the claim that they started a school in Taxila, in Kashmir? I'd like to know more about that.

Joseph: Yes there is. There has been some remarkable work done in Taxila by John Marshall. You can get his *A Guide to Taxila* and see that his archeological work has uncovered sufficient evidence that a Greek-style city was founded there; that's where they built monasteries, fortresses, and even started a kind of university in Taxila. You know Rod Wallbank, don't you? Well, he has the three-volume work of Marshall's that includes maps of the site, photos of Hellenic-style sculpture, Hellenic coins, artifacts galore. Give him a call; he'll be glad to share it with you. I imagine you are going to explore what Mortimer Wheeler said about Kandahar, Ai' Khanoum, Charsada, and Taxila. He said that Kandahar, "was a balanced Greek city with its writers, its philosophers, its teachers." I hadn't realized that there was an Indo-Graecia civilization flourishing at that time; it is something to marvel about.

Raymond: I'll give him a call; I'd love to see it. Now, let's turn to Nagarjuna and Pyrrhon. I enjoyed seeing that the dialectic was introduced into Indian and Buddhist thought through Pyrrhon. McEvilley argues that the dialectic has a long history of development among the Greeks but none prior to Nagarjuna. He argues that the Hellenics must have introduced it, since Nagarjuna's dialectic picked up at the stage of development of that of Sextus Empiricus and that it was brought to Taxila. He advances the idea that the Pyrrhonian arguments can be found before Alexander, in the writings of Eleatics—Academic or Platonic—and among the Cynic philosophers.

What amazed me was seeing the extraordinary similarity between Nagarjuna and Pyrrhon positions. To realize that these two thinkers were expressing the same doctrines, the same attitude, and even using the same metaphors and analogies to express their thought was eye opening. The recurrent use of the imagery of the rope that seems like a snake, the use of the smoke and fire image to explore causation in both traditions was significant. But for all that, it was even more surprising to realize that the very purposes of the dialectic were the same in both traditions, Nirvana for Nagarjuna and Ataraxia for the Pyrrhonians.

Say, Joseph, are you convinced, as I am, that there was this Greek influence on Buddhist or Indian logic before Alexander's conquests?

Joseph: Actually, you will find McEvilley's study of *Early Greek Philosophy and the Madhyamika* is part of a growing body of literature that argues for that issue. Given your interest you can also check on Richard H. Robinson's work, and don't ignore the insightful work of Alfonzo Verdu's on the dialectical aspects in Buddhist thought. You have a good mind for this kind of reflection, Raymond, so it is likely you are going to have to check out Sir William Tarn's claim that a Hellenistic dynasty was preserved throughout this region, and in those genuine *polis* cities were philosophers, teachers, stonecutters doing their thing. They even constructed amphitheaters for tragic and comic plays.

Raymond: Sometime I think it all borders on fantasy. I was taken into McEvilley's thought and more than once wondered whether this was some scholar whose imagination was greater than his research. However, Joseph, he opened up an issue I once wondered about but never pursued. I used to wonder if Plato's *Republic* might have influenced the great legendary King Asoka. He started a rational rule that historians and thinkers look upon with envy. I let that idea go as too far fetched only to find that McEvilley said that the edicts of Asoka were found in Kandahar carved in stone in Greek. Now you know there must have been a sizable Greek population for that kind of thing, right?

Joseph: True, and it seems that that cruel viper known as philosophy bit you. Why don't you tell me what you found that convinced you that the systems of Pyrrhon and Nagarjuna were not only similar but have the same strategy for achieving their philosophical goals?

Raymond: That's fair. I'll gladly do it as long as you remember to talk about the relationship that all this has to Plato. You promised and have yet to discuss it. Well, I was influenced by one argument that McEvilley put forward. It was so simple that I became convinced he was right about the essential identity of Pyrrhonism and Nagarjuna's Madhyamika Buddhism, and because of that he had a right to claim the Indo-Graceo thesis you just mentioned.

First, let me back up a bit and say that this Pyrrhonism grew out of a Stoic philosophy, and it reached its high point with Sextus Empiricus in the second century of our Common Era. During the same time Nagarjuna spent most of his life in Naagaarjunakonda and that city was in the orbit of Hellenistic influence. Actually, you know that they have found there many Graeco-Roman medallions and Buddhist Stupas that clearly show Greek artistic influences.

So much for that, but as I was saying, what convinced me that Nagarjuna was deeply influenced by the thinking of Sextus Empirircus was McEvilley's idea that whenever you find Nagarjuna difficult to follow, all you have to do is find the parallel idea being discussed in Sextus. I spent many an hour trying to figure out Nagarjuna and along comes this idea, so now I study Sextus and use that to cut through the difficulties I find in Nagarjuna. I struggled with his ideas of time and space, origination and destruction, motion and rest, substance and attribute, and never guessed that the same criticism runs through them all. It is that simple. The arguments against cause and effect are a kind of paradigm for all these pairs of ideas, so you can substitute any pair for cause and effect and you can see his criticism of them. When I saw that was true, I jumped for joy. I never suspected there was this kind of connection. To find that Robinson also saw this clearly was something I was really pleased to see. He said that you could substitute different terms or ideas within the same pattern in either Sextus or Nagarjuna. Here are important works that I needed to find and learn about and I didn't even know they existed.

Joseph: Hold it for a moment! Even if there is this kind of correspondence, are you willing to agree that the Nirvana of the Madhyamika is the same as that of Ataraxia for the Pyrrhonists? Are you willing to say that the Stoics, Cynics and the Pyrrhonists really had a spiritual life on the par with Nagarjuna? Have you become convinced that these Greek philosophers achieved the ideal of the Madhyamika? Now, you know that will need a bit of rewriting history won't it, Raymond?

Raymond: Yes, and what adds to my pain is a lot of confusion. Sure, I know that means I'm in a state of suffering. The cause of it is clear enough, and so, too, is the remedy, and it sure doesn't need an eight-fold path. It becomes a crazy question to even ask, but the logic of it is compelling. I'll state it loudly so it can penetrate deep into my mind, "Why am I still a Buddhist if I can do and get the same thing from Sextus Empiricus?" If they are doing the same thing, then the Pyrrhonian tradition was as much of a spiritual tradition as the Buddhist. This turns everything around. Surely, that means that the persecution and exile of non-Christian philosophers during and after the reign of Emperor Constantine brought about the end of all spiritual systems that competed with Christianity. However, the picture that our philosophers and historians have given us about these systems stresses only the logical character of their works and ignores this profound spiritual dimension. Frankly, it is a rip off.

Joseph: You do have the questions. Some have called the obliteration of the Hellenic culture genocide. I do think you are seeing the differences between religious belief and the cultivation of states of mind. But Raymond, are we to forget about the difference between Nirvana and Ataraxia? You've done your homework, you've studied it, it sure is important to you, so now wouldn't you like to share what you have seen?

Raymond: Well, to begin with, both systems of the dialectic are designed to remove consciousness from identifying with any conceptual structure and that includes both natural and philosophical languages, and to block the possibility of identifying with ontology. They both believe the unreflective imposition of language and its categories on experience forces experience into the categories of language for which it is totally unfitted. It creates all the delusions and with it all the sufferings that mankind experiences. Thus, when you realize this, then the very conditions for being upset and suffering are overcome. And I know it is not an easy and simple task to live without these impositions of thought upon experience. It takes courage and an inner determination to live without concepts, but the concept-free mind is the mind of the Buddha, enlightenment.

The idea that we can have a non-conceptual experience of the moment, without intense goal direction in life, and without emotional attachment is actually common to both Nagarjuna and Sextus. When the mind is suspended so that it neither affirms nor denies anything and recognizes nothing is more this than that, one reaches Epoche. What is that but a mind suspended from judging things as good or bad, right or wrong, and neither real nor unreal? Thus, the mind reaches silence (aphasia), freedom from all phenomenal influence (apatheia), and is no longer perturbed (ataraxia) so that each moment is lived without being either attached nor non-attached to anything. So, Joseph, is that not a fair picture of the problem before us?

Joseph: I am sure we can talk about this further and delve into the issue for more precision, but I have to say I enjoyed your summary. It is good to see that you too have found McEvilley and these other authors as important as I have. You presented your understanding clearly, and it reminded me of the days when you were at college exploring philosophy.

Raymond: It is your turn now, Joseph. I told you how this issue has influenced me so. Now, how about you? You must have gone further since I heard about how you tied together not the Madhyamika with Pyrrhonism as I did, but you went on to tie it into Plato. I thought that was weird; but knowing you, I wanted to hear from you what you have come to.

Joseph: First of all let me say that this study has had a major impact on my thinking and will undoubtedly influence my teaching of Plato and Buddhism. I'm not sure, as yet, in what way, but it will enter into my presentations. Before I explored these issues it never occurred to me that Pyrrhonism could be found in Plato's dialogues. I was really surprised to find it in Plato's *Parmenides*. Consider this idea for a moment: What if the basic theory of Pyrrhon has its equivalent in the thesis that Zeno presents in the *Parmenides*? Now just a moment, suppose we add another question? What if we find that very thesis of Zeno's that is discussed in depth in "Proclus' Commentary on Plato's *Parmenides*" shows its absurdity?

Raymond: Remind me, please, about Zeno's position. I can't recall it as accurately as I would like.

Joseph: That is fair, but before I spell it out let me remind you that the basic criticism of both Pyrrhon and Nagarjuna is that when the fundamental categories of our language are attributed to our experience, the result is a series of absurdities. The result of this critique is that we withdraw from mind-projections and become tranquil souls.

Zeno summarizes his view of the phenomenal world and concludes everything is both like and unlike. He expresses it simply, saying that if things are many, they are both like and unlike; and he then concludes that such a case is impossible "for the unlike cannot be like nor the like unlike." Socrates merely points out that there is nothing at all strange in "things that partake of both, become both like and unlike," but he adds it really would be a "wonder if anyone could show that the idea of like itself becomes unlike." You see, Raymond, he doesn't think it strange that when these categories are applied to the "many things," or to the appearances, that such consequences follow. Proclus goes on to show that not only these ideas of like and unlike but all the forms can, indeed, be mixed and partake of community with one another without becoming the other, for by partaking of the nature of the other they yet preserve their own nature. Proclus goes further and argues that the idea of like and unlike is in contraries and applies to four distinct levels. On the level of matter these contraries are destructive to each other and cannot coexist; on the level of the heavenly orbiting planets they coexist; on the level of souls they are separate while functioning together; and to intellect they are unified and are creative forces. Thus, Proclus shows that the argument of Zeno, and hence of Sextus, applies only to the phenomenal world, so that it is only valid if that is all there is to our existence, but since there is the intelligible, it lacks scope.

Raymond: That truly is surprising to me. I'm going to have to return to Plato's *Parmenides* and Proclus. I'm not even sure I can state what the consequences would be if what you say is true. I would like to sit on that for awhile and get back to you later on this one. I seem to be missing something.

Joseph: There is something more, something that I do believe you have not fully appreciated about the Platonic tradition. The difference between the Platonic tradition and those of Pyrrhonism, Stoicism, and the Cynic philosophies is that they do not pass through the Idea of the Good to reach their enlightenment, as the Platonic does. The Idea of the Good is the most brilliant light of Being that once experienced and understood becomes the proper object of the dialectic, which brings one to the Good or the One. Thus, the dialectic has a different function in each of these systems. Once you appreciate that difference, you may find it impossible to stay a Madhyamika.

Raymond: Now, that is something to say. I'll have to work on that idea.

So that is their essential difference.

Joseph: Yes, they have no room for the intelligible in their systems. It is somewhat difficult for some people to accept the idea that when the very nature of reality is perceived by the mind, which alone can see and know it, that it experiences a wondrous beauty, a perfection of beauty, which is the goal of those who seek to know the meaning of our existence.

Raymond: I guess I'm one of those. I can't believe that there really is that kind of thing. I always thought of it as a creation of Plato's active imagination. So I have been doing my yoga and got into Buddhism. In Buddhism, if you cut away the delusion there is only the unnameable and unspeakable. But you are saying there is a third thing, the intelligible, right?

Joseph: There are not two separate and different planes of existence, because the intelligible penetrates the world of appearances, of becoming; and those who recognize this are the ones who speak about a pure knowledge, justice, and temperance.

Raymond: That's where I stop. I can't believe there is any such penetration of these ideas. You believe these ideas have some kind of independent and essential existence, and I would say they are all relative to our experience.

Joseph: Well, that is what philosophy is all about, learning to see these things; and that is not easy because you can't perceive such things through the senses. And I imagine you would also say that each of these ideas only has its meaning in relation to its negation, and so you would suspend your judgment about their being real. Sure, but this can be said, however, as we were saying: the real can be experienced and it is called Being itself, or the Intelligible, or the Idea of the Good, or that most brilliant light of Being so that it is not merely or only relative to its opposite or its relational.

Raymond: Perhaps it is as you say, and perhaps not. I have an idea for our next coffee-talk. Let's invite a Pyrrhonist, a Zen Master, and a Parmenidean Platonist and get them to say hello to one another, and you and I can enjoy the discussion, ask a few questions, and learn what we can from them.

Joseph: Anything else?

Raymond: Yes. It would be interesting if a course were offered on this at your Golden West College. But where do you see all this going, Joseph? I can't even guess what the implications are.

Joseph: You like analogies, don't you? Well here is one for you to consider: If the magnificent Madhyamika Buddhism is transplanted Pyrrhonism and Sextus Empiricus, what would they have done if they had had Plato's *Parmenides* and Proclus' *Commentary* to meditate upon? Or, as Pyrrhonism is to Madhyamika Buddhism, so... what would be to Plato and Proclus?

Raymond: All I can say is that something would emerge that would be more profound, and it would have more far-reaching consequences on the spiritual life of man than anything I can imagine.

Bibliographical Sources from Thomas McEvilley

Dar, Saiphour Rachman. Taxila and Hellenism: architectural evidence: a new approach to the study of Gandara art, Saifur Rahman Dar. Lahore: [S.R. Dar?], 1976. 14p: ill., map; 25cm.

Frenkian, A. M. "Sextus Empiricus and Indian Logic," *PQ* (India) 30, no. 2 (1957): 123.

Gangadean, A. K. "Formal Ontology and the Dialectical Transformation of Consciousness," *Philosophy East and West* 29, no. 1 (January, 1979): 22.

Jones, Richard Hubert. "The Nature and Function of Naagaarjuna's Arguments," *Philosophy East and West* 28 (1978): 490-491.

Kalupahana, David J.*Buddhist Philosophy, A Historical Analysis*, Honolulu Hawaii: The University Press of Hawaii, 1976).

Marshall, John Hubert, Sir, 1876-1958. *Excavations at Taxila: the stupas and monasteries at Jaulian*, New Delhi.

Mates, Benson. Stoic Logic (Berkeley, California: University of California Publications in Philosophy, 1953).

McEvilley, Thomas. "Early Greek Philosophy and Madhyamika," Philosophy East and West 31, no. 2 (April, 1981): 141-164.

"Pyrrhonism and Madhyamika," *Philosophy East and West* 32, no. 1. : 3-35.

"Plotinus and Vijnanavada Buddhism," *Philosophy East and West* 30, no. 2 (April 1980): 181-193.

Plato. *Parmenides*. translated by H. N. Fowler, The Loeb Classical Library, 1970.

Proclus. *Proclus' Commentary on Plato's Parmenides.* translated by Glenn R. Morrow and John M. Dillon. Princeton University Press, 1987.

Robinson, Richard H.Early. *Madhyamika in India and China* (Delhi, 1976).
Stcherbatsky. *The Buddhist Conception of Nirvaana* (Leningrad, 1927), 187-188.
Sextus Empiricus. in four volumes. translated by The Rev. R.G. Bury. Harvard University Press. 1937.
Tarn, W. W. *The Greeks in Bactria and India* (Cambridge, 1951).
Verdu, Alfonzo. *Dialectical Aspects in Buddhist Thought* (Lawrence, Kansas: University of Kansas, 1974), 27-28.
Wheeler, Mortimer. *Flames Over Persepolis* (NY, 1968) *Rome Beyond the Imperial Frontiers* (London, 1954), 121.

Appendix 1: The Philosophical Midwife Talk Notes

In the Symmetry play, the philosophical midwifery (PMW) talk refers to board notes which are produced as a part of the performance. On these two pages is a reproduction of the talk notes for the philosophical midwifery talk upon which the play is based.

APPENDIX 1   177

The notes are broken into two parts to fit them on the pages with as large as possible a reproduction for this book. The original notes are on a flip chart 27" wide. The reader should be aware that these notes and drawings are valuable in keeping the talk concentrated on the problem and not on the relationship between the subject and the philosophical midwife.

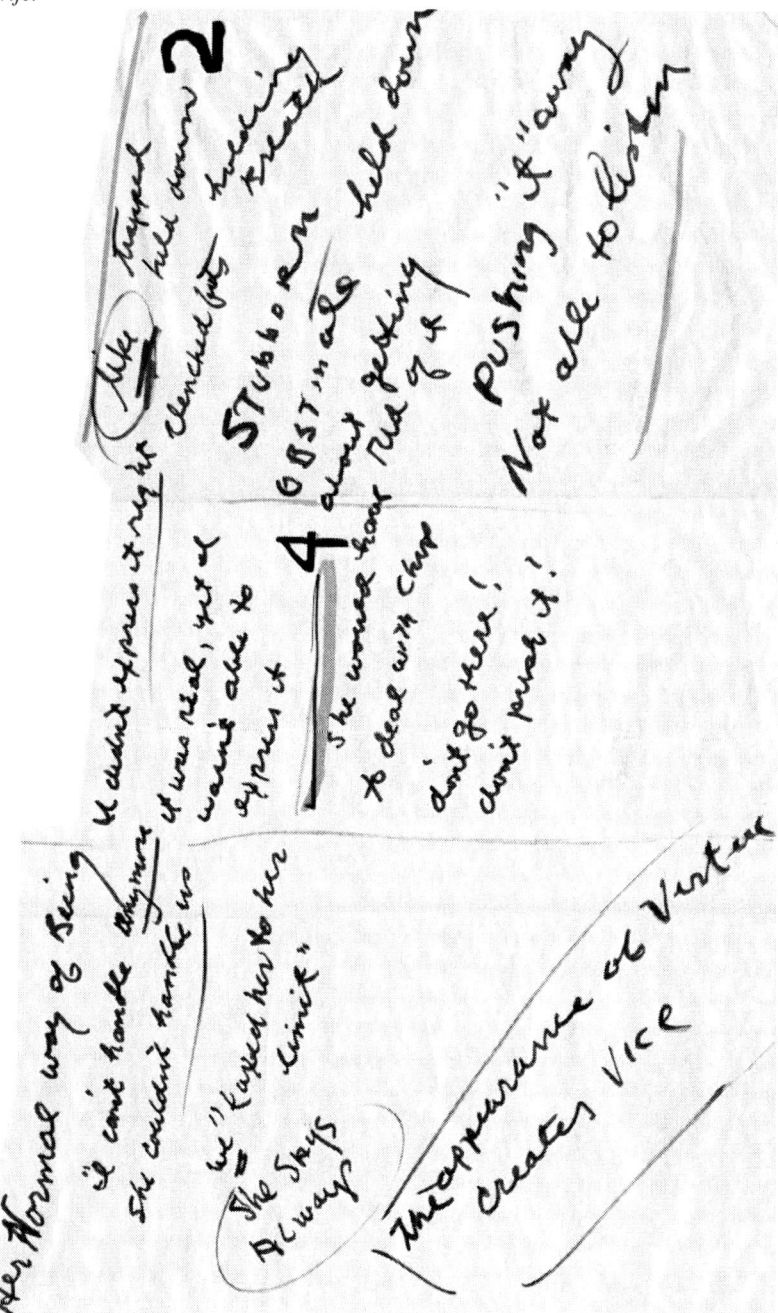

Appendix 2: Images in Words

These are alternate versions and added developments to some sections of the performed version of Symmetry presented in this book which the reader may find insightful.

Sophron: Languages that preserve their roots, cultures that preserve the roots and keep alive the roots of their language always have an edge on reflection because the images are alive and continuous. When you import language that has no image then you're literally in the realm of abstraction from experience. We are trying to reach a level of reflection that can more accurately describe our experience, and by searching for words that can vivify and enrich past memories we find more details surface from these past scenes. In this way, the possible parallels and similarities of both the past and its analogous situations become available for exploration and comparison.

Now the best way to see this–if you ever want to get a good chance– all it will take you is just a couple weeks to do this, and you'll never forget it. Get a book such as Creel's *Literary Chinese*. Why? He'll show you that the calligraphy that the Chinese use in their writing goes back to what are called the *shuo wên* which is the prior stage before the pen and the ink were developed where they used just a stylus and scratched symbols on the backs of tortoise shells, that's the origin of Chinese writing. If you go back to this primitive form of writing which you can see behind the calligraphy, you'll then see the images that are kept alive such as teaching. The word *teaching*: What is involved in teaching? In the Chinese character, it's a man with a child, the man is holding a stick illustrating something to the child.

(Note: For the following, the numbers refer to the characters drawn as Sophron speaks. See the graphics next.)

(1) Peace. What do we mean by peace? In Chinese there is absolutely no difficulty understanding what peace is, it's an open mouth with a rice plant next to it.

(2) This is very interesting. Think for the moment and try to come up with your idea of what this is.

(3) Now, in Chinese, this character is like something that flows and proceeds, like falling rain, not a storm, falling rain, like water in a waterfall, like cascading water, but not in any fury, just a natural flowing water, that's the character.

```
 和   氵 ─ 德 ─ 罒
 1    3    2    心
                   4
                   5
                   6
```

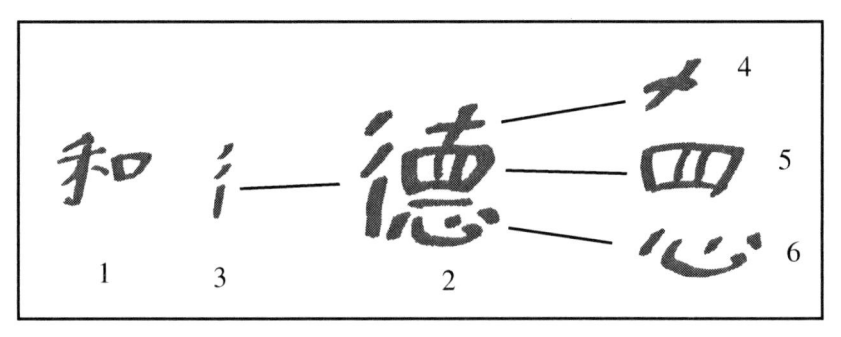

(4) This is used as a symbol for archery.

(5) So, this is stylized for this, the eye. And therefore it's written this way, stylized.

(6) If you went back far enough this would be the image of a heart, stylized, see? Stylized.

(2) Therefore, if you are able to naturally, with a certain ease and flow, directly, like hitting the mark, see into your heart. That's virtue.

They capture the process of being virtuous, to be able to see directly into your heart. Now, would you not agree, therefore, when you're talking to someone who's Chinese, or who knows Chinese, and uses the word virtue, they're going to use it in a different way than you are. You may try to figure out what it is by defining it. They can go in their language, since their language preserves the metaphors—these are metaphors—and they're alive. Therefore you can get an insight into language.

All you have to do if you want to use a Chinese dictionary is count the number of strokes, and that's the way their dictionaries are designed. So this would be one, two, three, four, five, six, seven, eight, nine, ten, eleven, twelve, thirteen, fourteen, fifteen. To look at this word, you'd look up all the words with fifteen strokes. Cause that's the way in which they catalogued things. Now, therefore any word at all, any word at all that you're interested in looking up, you'll always get a fundamental insight into what is behind the word pictured in Chinese. So what does that mean? Now, this is Latin—virtue—very few people know what they mean when they're talking about the word virtue. Suppose I put into it another word—which is English, which dates back to the Anglo Saxons, which literally means the same thing—excellence. Human excellence. What does that do? How is it different?

SOMEONE: It's understandable. It's closer to an image.

SOPHRON: Yeah, see, we can grasp behind that all kinds of images that we can use. Difficult to talk about the virtue of a horse, yet you can talk about an excellence of a working horse, different kinds of horses, can't you? You can talk about the virtue of a knife, depending upon what kind of a knife it is. What?! They don't lie. Oh, there's an excellence in certain kinds of knives that have been specifically designed to achieve certain purposes better than other knives. That's the virtue of a pruning knife. We don't talk that way, but that's the way our language guides us, and therefore, we're in total confusion. OK, try it. Frustration. What is it? What's the difference between frustration and closing down? See, the word frustration allows such a wide range that it's not usable, though you know it is some kind of distress, that's clear. We want to get away from that range of uses so that you can find something that is expressive of a person's experience.

Therefore, avoid Latin-rooted words, especially in this game, because in one's choice of words you will find rich metaphors and similes that keep alive and can communicate the depth of one's personal experiences. The reasons why the German nation as a people purged their language, periodically they want to purge their language and their dictionaries of non-German words to preserve that sense of keeping the basic metaphors alive in their culture. We don't. We take anything. Jeep, right? Xerox! Let's "Xerox" it. And that's the freedom in our language, a restriction in others, but each has its own purpose and serves a purpose depending upon your interests. So! See, we're here now.

DAVID: So, the word anguish is less broad.

SOPHRON: That's right. At first I'd be willing to use that and then see what's behind it. I'm not satisfied until the words reveal a specific particularity; or the specificity of one's experience. The more a person describes this experience in personal terms, the richer is their reflection and the closer they are able to reach meaning. And meaning is never on the surface, it is something that is behind it and is that which is responsible for the forms. A problem is a function of nature. Nature is the emergence of forms in our experience. Julie, you say you can't penetrate, are not able to perceive (reach) it, but in some way your mind can see and you're trying to focus your mind to see something that's just outside of your reach, you can't put your finger on it, it builds up an intense concentration, doesn't it? That's interesting.

When you are satisfied with a description of the state of mind that is behind the key words, then you can say what that is like; that's a simile. You can't get any precision in a simile that is too broad. It'll go too many places. That's a simile.

"None of us can understand ourselves, or anyone else, unless we give up or see through what we believe in. And if we can't do that, it is unlikely that we can reach a deeper understanding of anything else either."

Pierre Grimes
from *Is It All Relative?*

Other Works by Pierre Grimes

Journal Articles:

"Homer and the Struggle for Excellence." APPA Journal: Philosophical Practice Vol.1 No.1 (2005)

"Alcibiades: A Dialogue Utilizing the Dialectic as a mode of Psychotherapy for Alcoholism" Yale Journal: Quarterly Journal of Studies on Alcohol 22. (1961) 277-297.

"Vinodorus:: A Dialogue Exploring a Frame of Reference for Dialectic as a Mode of Psychotherapy in the Treatment of Alcoholism." Rutgers U. Press. Quarterly Journal of Studies on Alcohol 27 (1966):693-716.

A contiuing column and series of articles in *The Hellenic Chariot*, the journal of the Noetic Society, Inc., 1990--1995.

Books to Become Available in 2009

The Way of the Logos.
Return of the Gods: A Five-part Dialogue-play.

Conference Participation

"A Validation of the Grimes Dialectic as a Mode of Psychotherapy" 94th Annual Conference American Psychological Association Washington D.C., USA, August, 1986.

"Lecture and Demonstration of Philosophical Midwifery" The Philosophical Counseling Workshop Conference International Association of Philosophical Counseling & Enquiry, London, England November, 1996.

"The Emergence of the Pathologos in Dreams" Association for the Study of Dreams, 71st Annual American Philosophical Association Conference, Berkeley, California, July, 1996.

"Defining Philosophical Midwifery" American Society of Philosophical Counseling & Psychotherapy 72nd Annual American Philosophical Association Conference Berkeley, California, April, 1997.

"False Beliefs: The Pathologos in Philosophical Midwifery" American Society of Philosophical Counseling and Psychotherapy American Philosophical Association, Pittsburgh, Pennsylvania, April, 1997.

"A Study of Philosophical Midwifery and a Demonstration." Third International Conference on Philosophical Counseling New York, New York, August, 1997.

"The Moral Crisis in the Exploration of Philosophical Midwifery" Phaideia: Twentieth World Congress of Philosophy Boston, Massachusetts, August, 1998.

"Symmetry and the Origin of the Pathologos in Philosophical Midwifery" Pierre Grimes with Barbara Stecker, Fifth International Conference of Philosophy in Practice Wadham College, Oxford, England, July, 1999.

"Philosophical Midwifery: a New Paradigm." VIII International Symposium on Philosophy and Culture Russian Academy of Sciences, St. Petersburg, Russia, September, 2000.

"A New paradigm: A Hyperspace Model for Dialectical Philosophical Practice" Fourth Conference of Science and Consciousness Albuquerque, New Mexico April, 2002.

"The Process of Alienation and Transition in Dialectical Philosophical Practice" by Dr. Pierre Grimes, Presented by Dr. Regina Uliana, Eighth Conference of the International Society for the Study of European Ideas (ISSEI), Wales, England, July, 2002.

"Transcendentalism and Pragmatism in Dialectical Philosophical Practice" American Society for Philosophy, Counseling, and Psychotherapy 77th Annual American Philosophical Association San Francisco, California, March, 2003.

"Introduction and Demonstration of Philosophical Midwifery" Canadian Society for Philosophical Practice University of St. Paul, Ottawa, Canada, September, 2003.

"The Dialectical Philosophical Practice: A New Paradigm for Understanding Human Problems" XXIst World Congress of Philosophy Istanbul, Turkey, August, 2003.

"Homer and the Struggle for Excellence," International Association for Greek Philosophy First World Olympic Congress of Philosophy, March , 2004.

"Rational Structure of Pathologos Problems," Keynote Speaker, University of Liverpool Philosophy Conference, Liverpool, England, 2006.

"The structure of analogy in book six of Plato's Republic," Keynote Speaker, Symposium: "A Day with Plato," School of Economic Science, London, England, July, 2006.

"The Necessity of Dream Analysis in the Philosopher's art in Plato's Republic," Speaker and Demonstration, The First Prometheus Trust Conference, July 2006, Maidencroft Farm, Glastonbury, Somerset, England. Conference Theme: "Rebuilding Platonism, Mysticism, Scholarship, and Living," July, 2006.

In addition, Dr. Pierre Grimes has published papers in major journals and through electronic media. The interested reader is invited to visit

www.openingmind.com

www.platonicstudies.org

and/or to use a standard search engine to find this extensive body of work.